MW00723645

The Comeback from a Major Setback
By Maurice Williams

Published by Purpose Publishing
1503 Main Street #168 ✦ Grandview, Missouri
www.purposepublishing.com

ISBN: 978-0692363881

Copyright © 2015, Maurice Williams

Editing by: Rosalind Bauchum

Printed in the United States of America

This book, or parts thereof, may not be reproduced, stored
in a retrieval system, or transmitted in any form or by
means – electronic, mechanical, photocopy, recording, or
any other without the prior permission of the publisher.

All scriptures are taken from the King James Version, New
King James Versions of the Bible and The Message Bible.

Contents

Maurice Williams

Acknowledgements

To my children: Monique, Mikayla, Mishael, Menellus, and Haley. I would like to say; thank you guys again for your faithfulness, for being the pillars that upheld everything that was falling down around me. I want to say I love you. Thank you for taking heed to our teaching and instructions that helped the family and church ministry during the worse crisis of my life. You guys are the support system that I needed in order to make this comeback.

To my uncle Bobby Anderson, thank you for standing with me in ministry for over 21 years.

To Don Kinsey, Minister LaVonda Graham, Angela Collins, and Cathy Brown. You guys are the *awesome foursome* for the ministry. Thank you for all you've done. You know all things you do.

To all the members of Church Triumphant World Overcomers International; you are the greatest members in the whole wide world. Thank you for not leaving my side when leaving would have been the easiest thing to do, when it appeared that it was all over for the church ministry.

To my spiritual Father and Mother, Bishop Steve and Dr. Donna Houpe; thank you for your covering and for your prayers. I also would like to thank you for encouraging me to continue to fight the good fight of faith in every battle. Not to faint, loose courage, cave in or quit, because I have the victory through faith. Thank you for demonstrating to world of ministry how to make marriage and family a top priority.

Dedication

This book is dedicated to my beautiful wife, my best friend, the mother of my children; Lady Holly Williams. I want to say again that I love you, I appreciate you, I honor you.

Thank you again for saving my life, and for your encouragement and all your love. You were cheering for me to win, even when it looked as if I had lost the battle. You are my biggest cheerleader. Thank you for your leadership at home as well as the Church, especially when I was unable to do any formal everyday activities for two years. I dedicate this book to you

This book is in loving memory of my nephew/son, Kamal Bensahri, March 28, 1994 - May 27th, 2014, who encouraged me to write this book. The book is finished. Unfortunately, he will never have an opportunity to read it.

Maurice Williams

Honoring the Comeback

Apostle Larry B. Aiken
Memorial Church International
Kansas City, MO

Pastor Maurice Williams is an example to every believer and every child of God. The sickness he went through not only showed us the favor of God, but showed us the purpose of God for his life.

This man of God was so full of God's purpose but he refused to die. Even when the situation did not look good, he refused to die. When the odds were not in his favor and in the midst of it all, he chose to believe the report of the Lord.

I watched his wife, his family; his church and his faith bring him through to a place of destiny. If there was ever a time that the purpose of God was clear to myself and to others it was during the time we witnessed Pastor Williams with great faith and determination to walk in his God ordained and God given purpose.

Pastor Williams has been through brain surgery and a long rehabilitation. Williams has shown us that there is no end to God's purpose and God's faithfulness. It is with great anticipation that I look for extreme strength in the midst of this major comeback.

I'm grateful to God and I am on the winning team. Any team that Pastor Williams is on is a team of favor, purpose and true godliness.

Keeper of the Oil,

Apostle Larry B. Aiken

Apostle Halton "Skip" Horton
The Day Star Tabernacle International Church
Douglasville, GA

Pastor Maurice Williams is a wonderful man of God. He has overcome many afflictions, trials, and tribulations, but through it all, God has allowed him to write this book, "*A Come Back from a Major Set Back.*" It will take you through every walk of life including where you are in your relationship with Christ.

Scripture by scripture, this excellently written book propels you to learn who you are, who He is, and how to stand through every situation. Remember, "*when you have done all to stand; stand.*" This book will minister to your total being, mind, body, and spirit. It contains both natural and spiritual principles that will direct you to understand what God's purpose is for your life.

May God continue to bless you Pastor Williams as well as everyone who reads this book.

Love, Peace, and Increase,

Apostle Halton Horton

Apostle LeRoy McConico
Friendship Faith Ministries
Paola, Kansas

When hearing of Pastor Maurice Williams' sickness, Pastor Essie and I began to pray. A few days later, we went to the hospital to visit Pastor Williams. Many people including his wife, family and church family were praying for him, covering him with the blood of Jesus, and believing God for complete healing in his body. Before leaving, the Holy Spirit impressed upon my heart to tell his wife, "he shall live and not die and he shall come through this to declare the Glory of the Lord." I felt very strongly about that and God did just what he promised. Now Pastor Williams is back in the pulpit preaching the Word of faith like never before. To God be the Glory!!

Apostle Leroy McConico

Friendship Faith Ministries

Dr. Stephen Wiley, Pastor and Founder
Praise Center Family Church
Muskogee-Tulsa Ok

When I think of Pastor Maurice Williams I am reminded of Joel 2:25-27, " *And I will RESTORE TO YOU the years that the locust hath eaten....AND YOU SHALL EAT IN PLENTY AND BE SATISFIED, AND PRAISE THE NAME OF THE LORD YOUR GOD, that hath dealt wondrously with you; and my people shall never be ashamed. And ye shall know that I am in the midst of Israel and that I am the Lord your God, and none else: and my people shall never be ashamed.*

The locusts are the devourers that come in to steal, and eat-up, and rob us of God's blessing. But glory be to the Father for He is a restorer. Satan tried to rob Pastor Williams of his life and ministry, tried to eat-up his finances, and to steal friends and relationships. But God said, "I will restore." As Pastor Williams trusted God to restore- it is very evident that as he stood, and continues to stand, that God IS dealing wondrously with him, his family and ministry. I am witness to his restoration and COME BACK.

Pastor Maurice Williams is walking in Isaiah 61:7 - "Instead of your shame you shall have DOUBLE HONOR, and instead of confusion they shall rejoice in their portion. Therefore in their land they shall possess DOUBLE; everlasting joy shall be theirs."

13

Dr. Stephen Wiley, Pastor and Founder
Special Advisor to the President
Assistant Professor of Religion
Bacone College-Muskogee OK

Pastor Frank Thompson
Harvest Church
St. Louis, MO

In all the years of critical situations having to do with major strokes and aneurysms, I have only seen a few people who survived and thrived. My own father died of a major stroke, so when we got the news of our friend's stroke, we knew only God could bring him back and cause him to recover. We immediately left St. Louis to travel to the hospital and here is what we found upon our arrival. Hope against hope! There was a waiting room full of Pastor Williams' church members and friends waiting in hope, and believing God for a miracle. There was no shortage of the tubes and monitors connected to his body and the circumstances looked grave to say the least. All we could do was pray, as if that was not enough. We cannot say enough about how God gave his wife Holly the strength and the resolve to trust Him anyway. Now fast forward to where Pastor Williams is now, and you will only be able to declare that a bona-fide miracle took place. Even now as we look back, we can see both the love of God and the faith of the people that stood by him. However, what sticks out to me the most is the power of hope, for "hope maketh not ashamed."

Thankful for my friend,

Pastor Frank Thompson

Apostle Keith Wesley, Sr.
New Life in Christ International Ministries
Grandview, MO

The scripture in Ephesians 6:10 says, finally, my brethren, be strong in the Lord, and in the power of his might. When God tells us this it's an indication that we will have some major fights in this walk as believers. Sometimes it is, in our minds, unwarranted pain or it has a "why me" feeling that we go through. However, in the ultimate analysis of our personal situations, God's word teaches us to be strong in the Lord! Our strength is really HIs grace and His grace is released in measures that account for the need of the moment.

Pastor Maurice Williams has gone through one of the most catastrophic times a man and his family could go through. His pain was not only the church, but his family and his personal health. If anyone I know is a modern day "Job", it is this man!

This book "*The Comeback from a Major Setback*", will chronicle his journey that took him from a high place to a very low place to bring him back to a sure place by God's grace! I urge you to read this book so that you can understand that with God's strength you can face all your tests and trials and end up being conformed to the image of our Lord Jesus Christ!

Thank you, Pastor Maurice for allowing God to lead you to write these words. I believe it will edify many and strengthen all of us in the faith.

Godspeed,

Apostle Keith Wesley, Sr.

Bishop Eric Morrison
Kingdom Word Ministries
Kansas City, MO

Greetings in the name of our Lord and Savior Jesus Christ!

What an honor it is to give a voice to such an incredible act of God in a great man of God. Pastor Maurice Williams from the time that I met him has always been a man of faith who without fear has had to face many challenges and through the power of the Holy Ghost has always came through. But when I got the call that he was going to have surgery because of a aneurysm on his brain, we knew then this would totally be a move of God in his life.

Now here we are several months later, surgery, physical therapy, prayer, faith and love and Pastor Williams back standing, talking, preaching and teaching all over again because the hand of God being all over his life and his family. Let me just say, how can anyone read this book and not be completely convinced that after a MAJOR SETBACK they will not have a MAJOR COMEBACK .

God bless you Pastor Williams!

Love you,

Bishop Eric D. Morrison.

Pastor Dewayne Freeman
Spirit of Faith Christian Center
Temple Hills, MD

In Pastor Maurice William's new book, "The Comeback from a Major Setback," he shares how to bounce back from the devastation of a setback. He shows that God does not change His mind in the midst of a storm whatever He has planned and predestined for you before the storm He will not change during or after the storm. So if you are in the midst of a faith challenge and in the natural it looks like there is no hope, and you've been saying God where are you and do you really love me, be encouraged by Pastor Maurice Williams' testimony and don't give up because God has No respecter person, what God does for one He will do for another. All God require of you is that you be not weary in well doing, hold fast to His Word and you will reap too and Pastor Williams' book will show you how to do just that. This is a must read.

Min. Dewayne Freeman
Associate Pastor

Pastor Maurice Williams in the hospital
August 16, 2012

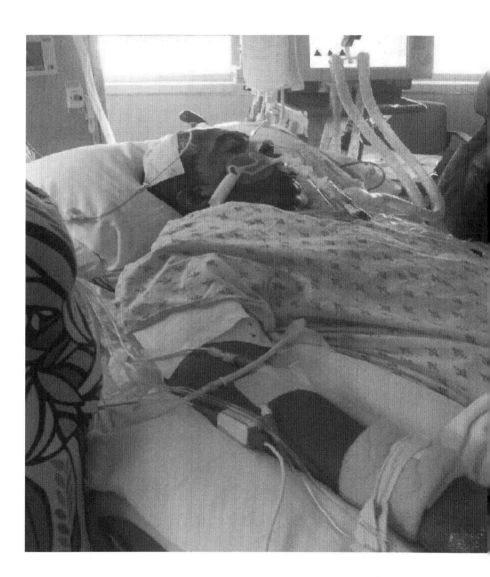

Preface

Tony D. Cobbins, Senior Pastor
Canaan Worship Center
Kansas City, Missouri

What do you do when you go from being a vigorous and energetic "go getter" one day and a long-term hospital patient the next? What do you do when you are the senior pastor of a thriving and growing church, and all of a sudden you are relegated to literally watching your congregation whittle down to a few faithful members? What do you do when you are faced with challenges in every area of your life with regards to faith, family, and finances? The average person would totally fall apart. The average person would throw in the proverbial towel. The average Christian would likely bring up a railing indictment against God. Pastor Maurice Williams is not the average person. Pastor Maurice Williams is a man of extraordinary faith and determination.

As a lifelong friend of Pastor Williams, I have witnessed him go through many challenges in his life, some of which had the potential to totally deplete him of hope and or joy of life. Nothing could have been more challenging than the day Pastor Williams was rushed to the hospital by ambulance after suffering a life threatening aneurysm. August 16th, 2012 is a day that I will never forget. When I received the call, informing me that Pastor Williams had been rushed to the hospital I immediately began to pray. Suddenly God gave me a very settling peace. The peace that God gave me was further fortified once I entered the emergency room where Pastor Williams was being attended. Although for the most part he was semi-unconscious, he was able to respond to my voice. I knew immediately that God was up to something wherein only He would be glorified at the outcome of this ordeal.

Now, here it is two years later, the one many thought was facing certain death is alive, well, and getting better. The ministry many had counted out is bouncing back and is still the "Church Triumphant!" What can be accredited for such remarkable recovery? The recovery can be attributed to Pastor Williams' unwavering faith in the supernatural power of God. Pastor Williams has a story to tell. He has a testimony to share. This is his story. This is his testimony of how he experienced a major "Setback" only to have God to lift him and put him on display as a victorious "Comeback."

If you are in the midst of what you perceive to be a major setback, you are going to be blessed and encouraged by what Pastor Williams has to share with you through the pages of this book regarding what it means to have "Comeback" faith.

Tony D. Cobbins, Senior Pastor
Canaan Worship Center
Kansas City, Missouri

Foreword

Bishop Clarence Williams Jr.
Living Word International Ministries

We all have challenges in life that seem to overwhelm us, suddenly they come upon us, leaving you speechless and numbed by it surprise attack. In this life bad things happen to good people, these things are out of our control leaving you helpless and totally defenseless of its aggressive and vicious acts. The question asks "What do you do, when you do not know what to do." How do you handle life challenges when you are not prepared for them? After hope has given up on you do you still hope, or where is the strength to get up when life knocks you down. This is a story about a man facing life challenges head on never wavering his faith in God but only believe in Him who began a good work in him was able to perform it to the very end. James said, *"My brethren, count it all joy when you fall into various trials, knowing that the testing of your faith produces patience. But let patience have its perfect work, that you may be perfect and complete, lacking nothing. If any of you lacks wisdom, let him ask of God, who gives to all liberally and without reproach, and it will be given to him."* ***James 1:2-5 (NKJV)"*** Pastor Maurice applied these scriptures and the outcome is amazing.

I encourage you to read this book of God's restoration power over this man life; it is truly a book that will help you when life challenges you. I have known Pastor Maurice Williams for a long time, his labor and love for God and the Church is without question. What happens to his life is no less than a miracle, I know this book had to be written by this man for such a time as this for others to be inspired and strengthen by one man's testimony of a mighty God who restores lives. Pastor Williams' tragedy to triumph will leave you with no doubt of the power and love of God. What he endured will strengthen your faith and brighten your hope in the Lord Jesus Christ and your Christian walk.

Bishop Clarence Williams Jr
Pastor

Introduction

This book is written and dedicated to all those in the body of Christ who have had setbacks in their lives; and now it seems difficult or in some cases impossible for you to get back on the road to purpose and destiny. My assignment is to deliver this written message to every believer and regardless of the setback; God has not changed his mind concerning His purpose and plan for your life. Your setback, is only a setup that God is going to use and bring you to bigger, better, and greater things. I would like to remind everyone that God is still good even when life seems bad. If you are facing a hopeless situation this book is for you.

Sometimes we can become blindsided by trials, tribulations, and unexpected falls in life. If you haven't experienced any of these, just keep on living! Some things will come and knock you to your knees. I don't care how strong or how spiritual you are. I am speaking from experience, by the grace of God, you can get back up to begin again. There is still a purpose for you after having a fall. Come go on a journey with me leading up to; and after a horrific incident that happened to me.

In June of 2012, I had a colonoscopy. Before the doctor performed the procedure, I explained to him that my feet were swelling. So the doctor who performed the procedure ordered a cat scan to make sure everything was alright. The scan came back negative. The reason why it was negative, the doctor did not put in the examination order for me to receive an injection of dye. If this had been done the strain on the undeveloped blood vessel would have been detected, rather than the surgeons having to literally open my skull to repair the aneurysm a couple months later.

The second week of July 2012, I attended the annual Covenant Alliance of Ministries, (C.A.M.) Conference hosted by Bishop Steve and Dr. Donna Houpe, in beautiful Branson Missouri. I contemplated whether I should attend because of swollen feet. I bought sandals in a larger shoe size, so I could attend the conference in spite of my swollen feet. We left home and drove three hours to the meeting in Branson, Missouri. I wore my sandals to each session because I didn't want to miss a word that my Bishop had to say. The same month, July 2012, my first cousin suffered with a brain issue. In addition, another cousin had an issue of the brain the following year in 2013. The only thing that saved his life is he woke up out of his sleep.

In medical terms, this is known as a form of stroke. A better understanding of this would be a rupture or an aneurysm. It is abbreviated AVM. An AVM is bleeding on the brain after a blood vessel ruptures. The doctors concluded their study of what happened to me was related to a genetic birth defect. I was a walking time bomb; very few people survive this type of stroke. If the aneurysm had occurred while traveling on the highway going to or returning from Branson Missouri; no doubt I would have died. On August 18, 2012 my wife and I were scheduled to move our youngest daughter (Haley) to Manhattan, Kansas to begin her freshmen year at Kansas State University. If the aneurysm had occurred on the highway going to or returning from Manhattan, Kansas; no doubt I would have died. On August 16, 2012, I suffered an Arteriovenous Malformation of the brain. I believe that God kept me from doing any traveling to save my life.

There are some things that I know now that I probably would have never known had it not been for the AVM. There are some things that you don't learn or receive except by having an experience. No one will be able to discredit your testimony. Everyone will conclude that God almighty is the only one that is able to perform this kind of miracle.

I've overcome the AVM and it was a near death experience. I am still here and I'm still alive! If you ever want to see a living, walking, talking, contemporary miracle of today, just look at me! Yes, I am still in recovery mode but I am walking out my healing deliverance daily! I didn't die. My story is to inform the body of Christ that there is life after having a fall. I could have looked at my situation two ways; one as an opposition or two, as an opportunity. I chose to look at it as an opportunity.

Just because you are struggling, does not mean you are failing. Every great success requires some kind of struggle to get there. Opportunity always comes with opposition.

I look at the fall as a reset button for me to start over and begin again. *"Better is the end of a thing than the beginning."* Ecclesiastes 7:8 KJV. The AVM restoration is a death, burial and resurrection process for me.

Maurice Williams

Chapter 1
This is my Story

On August 16, 2012, I was not sick; my blood pressure was not high. That day my wife planned to spend the day with her mother. My mother-in-law has dementia. Lady Holly tried and tried to get in contact with her stepfather to let him know that she was on her way to their home. Holly could not get in contact with her stepfather so she said to me; "I'm going to spend the rest of the day with you." Ten minutes later, it happened; the blood vessel ruptured in my brain. I vomited up a bloody substance. Had it not been a bloody substance, I probably would have remained at the house. As a man, I was determined not to go to the hospital, but because of the bloody substance, I knew this was something very serious. So I said, "I better go to the hospital."

I felt the pain the second time from the rupture. I began to yell with a loud voice, "God you're still good". In spite of what was going on, I began to give God praise. That's all I knew to do at that moment. I started doing what I've been preaching to others. When your back is against the wall, take time to break out into a praise. I have said to others; whenever you get in trouble, give God praise!

While in the back of the ambulance, I didn't know exactly what was going to happen to me. Different thoughts crossed my mind, but I knew I would return back home one day. As I began to praise God, I began to relax and I became calm. I had no fear whatsoever. I began to speak to myself in psalms, hymns and spiritual songs; *making melody in my heart to the Lord. Giving thanks always for all things unto God and the father in the name of our Lord Jesus Christ.* Ephesians 5:20.

I continued to praise God until I went into a state of unconsciousness. I know you are asking; how could you praise God at a time such as this. I understood one thing, that my situation could have been worse. I always say; there is nothing that is so bad, that it can't be worse. I began to praise God that my situation was as well as it was. I've learned how to praise God when things are going good and when things are going bad. *I will bless the Lord at all times and his praise shall continually be in my mouth* Psalms 34:1. When the squeeze is on, whatever is in you will be the first thing that will come out of you. This is why I could praise God. I had praise on the inside of me.

When my wife called 911, the paramedics were right down the street from our home. I believe God had them in place just for me. If my wife had left me at home to care for her mother, you probably would not be reading this book. God fixed it that my wife would be home with me on this particular day. When I arrived at the Menorah Medical Center in Overland Park, Kansas, their emergency staff could only relieve the blood that was filling my brain. They were unable to perform the brain surgery. Later that evening I transferred to the University of Kansas hospital, for the brain surgery. I was in the hospital fifty-seven days. My medical bills were well over half a million dollars. I was placed on a ventilator and a tracheotomy had to be performed.

While I was lying there, the doctors discovered in my blood work, that I had a traveling blood clot. The doctors had to monitor me around the clock to make sure the clot didn't travel to my heart. Miraculously the doctor did a procedure through my legs and the blood clot dissolved.

Dr. Abraham informed my uncle, Minister Sam Anderson; the only way that I would come through this is that I would have to be a man of faith. If I were going to live, it would have to be up to me. Another factor he said, was whenever the hospital receives a 911 call such as this, in most cases the individual is already dead.

My good friend Pastor Tony Cobbins came to the hospital and comforted my wife and daughters bringing a little humor to the situation. That is just my relationship with him. He told my girls; "you know, your father wouldn't want you crying like this." Your dad is back there resting and gathering material so when he does come through this, he's going to preach it."

One Sunday morning, one Pastor called and said; "Pastor Maurice Williams?" I replied; "this is he." Then he said these shocking words to me; "you might as well give up, because you will never rebound from this brain injury." I said to him; "the devil is a liar." I got off the phone and the Holy Spirit took me to Proverbs 24:16. It says *"A just man falleth seven times and riseth up again: but the wicked shall fall into mischief. "* The Holy Spirit told me to put my eyes on the promise of rising up again". This is how I arrived to the title of this book, **"The Comeback from A Major Setback"**.

There are several people in the Bible that experienced a fall and still fulfilled the will and purpose of God on their lives.   There were men like David, Moses, Sampson, Peter, Thomas, and Job. God's grace is greater than any fall. His grace will restore greater than before. Our God is not a God of a second chance, but a God of another chance.

Men look at the exterior of things, to make assumptions to come to conclusions. *"But the Lord said unto Samuel, look not on his countenance, or on the height of his stature, because I have refused him: for the Lord seeth not as man seeth; for man looketh on the outward appearance, but the Lord looketh on the heart",* I Samuel 16:7.

If anyone would look at my situation from the appearance of reality, they would conclude that my future didn't look much promising whatsoever. However if you know the truth, the future is not far away at all. Your future is on the inside of you. *"The word is nigh thee, even in thy mouth, and in thy heart: that is the word of faith which we preach."* Romans 10:8.

Whenever a fall is spoken of in the body of Christ, it is always interpreted as some kind of sexual immorality. A fall is anything that sets you back in life. It could be a divorce, a death, adultery, an unplanned pregnancy, bankruptcies, untimely foreclosure, business closures, a repossession, child molestation, rape, incarceration, debt, etc. *"being confident of this very thing that he which began a good work in you will perform it until the day of Jesus Christ"* Philippians 1:6. You can make a comeback.

It didn't surprise God that you suffered a fall. He saw the fall in eternity, and provided grace for that fall, so you would be able to get back up and begin again. This is why God never counts you out!

It is not over until God says it is over. Your setback is only positioning you for restorations, and future blessings of manifestations. When you see through the eyes of God, you are looking by revelation. You will see things that have been veiled. This makes it very easy to believe. Our design by God is to believe what we see. God is the most purposeful being there is. He has a purpose and a plan for you. If he didn't have a plan for you He never would have created you.

This AVM or stroke may be the worst thing that I have ever encountered. It has altered my life completely. This alteration is also bringing me into my next dimension. If this had not happened, maybe I wouldn't be on the search for the next dimension.

I've done my homework on this. Here are some statistics that will blow your mind. There are 795,000 new and recurrent strokes each year[1]. Someone in the United States has a stroke every 40 seconds. Stroke is the third leading cause of death in America. Stroke is the third leading cause of long-term adult disability. Approximately 160,000 people die from a stroke every year. In addition, another 5.5million, survivors continue to suffer after having a stroke. One out of every 10 families are affected by are stroke.

The American Stroke Association definition says a stroke occurs when a blocked or burst blood vessel interrupts blood flowing to the brain. A stroke is caused by a weakness in blood vessel walls. This vulnerability present from birth or from uncontrolled high blood pressure eventually can cause a blowout in the vessel. The blood will hemorrhage or leak out into the brain. Some of the most devastating elements of a stroke occur in its aftermath. Some of those elements are silence, paralysis, the inability to perform ordinary routines. These are some of the profound aftershocks of a stroke:

- Silence or the inability to speak
- Paralysis of body parts
- Loss of Self-esteem
- Excessive crying
- Withdrawal

- Excessive or lack of sleep
- Loss of interest
- Inability to concentrate
- Depressive thoughts.

There is good news regarding strokes! With proper care, knowledgeable and rehabilitation, most stroke victims can return home and resume their lives. By the grace of God, there is life after having a stroke. My wife and children were my support system for me to resume everyday life. If you are planning to make a comeback and resume everyday life, you will need to surround yourself with great people.

I was down so low that it looked impossible for me to get back up. One day I sat down on my sofa to finish the writing of this book. I turned on the TV and there was a group of people singing this song. Some of the lyrics to the song were" You ain't seen your best days yet!" In spite of the setbacks and the disappointments that I've had, I embraced the words of the song because it was a prophetic message to me.

Another pastor said to me "If I were you, I wouldn't even try to pastor again." "I would just let it go." The pastor continued, "God will understand if you do this." I believe that the pastor was being sympathetic because of my situation. The pastor is not me, nor does he know the call of God on my life. At the end of those 57 days spent in the hospital. God brought me back to finish the assignment He has given me. That assignment is to sound the alarm; Jesus is on his way back to rapture his church. This assignment is my purpose. I couldn't die because my assignment was not complete. What many don't know is where there is purpose there is life. I believe that the rest of my life will be the best of my life, fulfilling the purpose of God.

When I was released to go home from the hospital, I will admit I wasn't motivated to preach or pastor anymore. I wasn't excited about anything spiritual. It seemed as if all my dreams, visions, and aspirations died. My thoughts at that time were only to get well. I wasn't trying to get well so I could get back to the pulpit. I was trying to get well so I could just live a normal life. Sickness is not the will of God, but healing and divine health are. *"Beloved I wish above all things that thou mayest prosper and be in health even as thy soul prospereth."* III John 2.

Upon my return home from the hospital I was still struggling with my equilibrium. I suffered with vertigo. I couldn't even gather my words to pray, certain things I couldn't even remember. There were times I didn't even know what day it was. There are many scriptures that I knew, but I couldn't find them when I would open the bible. I would have to go to the table of contents to find what I wanted. This was truly hard for me. Often I would find myself crying because of this. So as a response, I memorized all the books of the Bible.

Thoughts of resigning from the ministry flooded my mind. It would be very difficult for me to pastor when everything in sight was spinning around. I concluded that the best thing for everyone would be for me to just resign.

My aunt Luvenia Carr, (Aunt Tiny) would call me and say, "You've got to be patient. I know it's hard for you to just sit and not do anything, but during this season in your life, that's what you're going to have to do." She would come to the hospital and shave me. She told me about her pastor Dr. C.L. Bachus, of the Mt. Zion Baptist Church, Kansas City, KS, who was diagnosed with throat cancer, and how he was unable to preach for two years. God has healed him and he's back preaching stronger than before. During this season of my life, I was unable to do anything physically. The enemy would try and plant defeated thoughts of giving up in my mind. I had enough word in me to know that these were not the thoughts of Jesus. I would cast down those negative thoughts and I would turn around and get in agreement with the word of God, that *by His stripes I am healed.* This was my prayer. This wasn't a long prayer, but it was a prayer of faith. *"All things are possible to him that believeth."* When I put my focus on purpose, I began to get motivated again.

I knew at age of thirteen, that one day I would preach the gospel. I really wanted to be a rock star, but in the back of my mind I knew God had his hand on me to preach his word, and to show many the way to a better life. This is my passion and I began preaching at age 19. I have had several falls, but because of purpose, I kept getting up reaching for destiny. *"A just man falleth seven times and riseth up again."* In order for me to proceed forward, I'm forgetting all the negative things behind me. *"I press toward the mark for the prize of the high calling of God in Christ Jesus."* Philippians 3:13-14.

No matter what has gone wrong in your life, God is working everything out that is best for you; by bringing the good out of every bad situation. God has not changed his mind concerning his purpose for your life, *for the gifts and the callings of God are without repentance."* Romans 11:29.

You may be saying after all I've been through and all the things I've done, how can God have a purpose for me? *"In whom also we have obtained an inheritance, being predestinated according to the purpose of him who worketh all things after the counsel of his will."* Ephesians 1:11.

I was down, but I got back up! I had no ideal of the strength that was on the inside of me. By faith, I had to believe that God put within me His strength to begin again. After experiencing the fall, thoughts would fill my mind that God's plans and purpose for my life had changed. Had God changed his plan and purpose for my life? What shall I do then? Where do I go from here? Is it all over?

Several pastors from all different denominations, who heard about my situation here in Kansas City, would tell me to go and apply for disability benefits. They advised me to get on a fixed income and receive a check each month for life, because I had gone beyond the point of no return. I would tell them that God is my source not disability benefits, because I will not always be like this. A monthly disability check cannot finance the vision for me and my family.

I had to research the scriptures for God's promises to assure me that God had not changed His mind about the plans and purpose for my life. I would ask God, what's next for me? Where do I go from here? One scripture that I embraced was Malachi 3:6 says *"For I am the Lord I change not."* Another scripture I held on to was James 1:17; *"Every good gift and every perfect gift is from above and cometh down from the Father of lights, with whom is no variableness, neither shadow of turning."* Another scripture was Hebrews 13:8; which says *"Jesus Christ the same yesterday and today, and forever."* Psalm 89:34, my covenant will I not break nor alter the thing that is gone out of my lips.

The brain aneurysm was sent to abort my purpose. If your faith is shaky, there will not be any manifestation. Regardless of all that I've been through, I know now, more than ever, that God has not changed his mind concerning his plans and purpose for my life.

God is redeeming the time that I've lost and He is bringing me to full destiny. I am right on schedule for the purpose He has promised. *I know the thoughts that I think toward you saith the LORD thoughts of peace and not evil to give you an expected end."* (Jeremiah 29:10-11), He hasn't forgotten about me

Chapter 2
Why Did This Happen To Me?

If you have had any church affiliation, no doubt you have heard the expression never question God? Because God is sovereign and He can do whatever He pleases. What people don't know is, God is only as sovereign as His word. People say God is the reason for all that happens in our lives.

God has predestinated each of us, and our lives have been planned by God before we were ever born. So the thing that happens to us whether they are good or bad is a direct or indirect result of predestination.

I was talking with a young man who told me he believes that he was destined for hell. He was the oddball of the family. He also told me that he didn't expect anything good to happen for him because it was the will of God for things to be this way for him. He told me this with tears in his eyes.

I want to go on record and say that God is good. He is loving and merciful. God has provided good things for everybody. He doesn't have picks and chooses. He doesn't choose to bless some and not bless others. *"Oh give thanks unto the Lord for He is good for his mercy endureth forever."* Psalms 107:1. God is good all the time and all the time God is good. God is love.

I know there are those who are sick and others are in good health. Some people are rich and others live in poverty. There are no respecter of persons with God, but God is a respecter of faith. God is not moved by your tears or your needs; he is only moved by your faith. I know this is difficult to except but it is truth.

Matthew 6:33 says; *"But seek ye first the kingdom of God and his righteousness; and all these things shall be added unto you."* The kingdom of God is not a lottery system that some win and some don't. The kingdom of God is God's way of doing things. If anyone releases their faith in Christ they have access to His grace. God is in the blessing business, he wants us all to win.

I don't believe that many understand the predestination of God. God doesn't pick out who he is going to save and reject others so that they will be eternally lost. "*The Lord is not slack concerning his promise as some men count slackness, but is long suffering to us not willing that any should perish but all should come to repentance*." II Peter 3:9. This is the will of God that no one is eternally lost. Now we know that not everyone will be saved, because not everyone will accept Jesus.

I was asked to give the eulogy of a young man that was a drug dealer. He was a victim of a drive by shooting. At the funeral service, his family and friends gave tributes of his life. Many of them said that God was sovereign. They also said that God works in mysterious ways, so therefore, it was the will of God that this young man would die this way and that all things work together for the good of them that love God.

I stood and gave the eulogy. I said first of all, God is loving and merciful. A Holy boldness came upon me; I said God is not a killer. Neither did He do a drive by shooting to end this young man's life. It was not God's will for this young man to die this way. This was not the will of God. There is nothing mysterious about God. Mark chapter, 4:11 says *"it is given unto you to know the mystery."*

If you develop a relationship with God, you can ask Him the reason why things happen. He can reveal to you the reason why. *"The secret things belong unto the Lord our God; but those things which are revealed belong unto us and to our children forever, that we may do all the words of the law."* Deuteronomy 29:29. I also believe there are some things that we will not know until we get to heaven. In this case, the young man opened the door to the spirit of death when he began selling drugs. No one can put the blame on God. This was not God's will.

If you understand the word of God you will also know the will of God. God's grace is greater than any fall. God's grace is so amazing that it can bring good out of every bad mistake. God can use all the bad you've gone through and get glory from it. *"God is your shield and your exceeding great reward."* Genesis 15:1. A shield represents protection. If bad things have happened to you know this, the bad had to go through the shield in order to get to you. If the "bad" passed through your shield, God allowed it to happen. If God allowed it to happen, get ready. He's about to bring good from it. Since it happened to you, it is because God has and sees a bigger plan for you!

No matter how bad the fall, God can still bring good out of it. God is working out a plan you can't see with your natural eyes. His plan for your life is perfect and generational. I believe it has some sort of global connection. God has a global vision; his plan is to connect you with others. This connection has the hook-up with those on the global scale. This plan is not just for you and your family. God's plan is for you to become a blessing to others. God said *"I will bless you and make your name great and you shall be a blessing."* I know that all looks hopeless at this very moment, but God has already paved the path for your return from the fall.

His plan is perfect and it will bring you to destiny. Yes God could have prevented the bad from happening to you, the question remains why did this happen? There is a reason why it happened. It didn't look good for Joseph the day his brothers cast him in the pit and sold him to the Ishmaelite traders. It was not coincidental the Ishmaelite traders were traveling that way. Relocating Joseph down into Egypt was the plan of God. It didn't look like it but it was; God saw the bigger picture because he had a bigger plan.

"And all the souls that came out of the loins of Jacob were seventy souls: for Joseph was in Egypt already. And Joseph died, and all his brethren, and all that generation. And the children of Israel were fruitful, and increased, abundantly, and multiplied, and waxed exceeding mighty; and the land was filled with them." Exodus 1:5-7.

Sometimes God may have to bring you into destiny a different route from the way you have planned. Before it's all over, you may be kicking and screaming, because it was not the way you planned things to happen. Remember, God knows how to bring you to destiny In spite of your fall. He sees a bigger picture and He has a bigger plan.

The Ishmaelite traders were passing by; so the brothers pulled Joseph up and lifted him up out of the pit, and sold him for 20 shekels of silver. *"And they took Joseph to Egypt."* Genesis 37: 28 NKJV.

God's purpose was to relocate all the Israelites, down into Egypt. God made a promise to Abraham.   He said to Abram; *"know certainly that your decedents, will be strangers in a land that is not theirs, and will serve them, and they will afflict four hundred years. And also the nation whom they serve I will judge; afterward they shall*

45

come out with great possessions." Genesis 15: 13-14 NKJV.

God's purpose goes far beyond Joseph. Joseph was in a foreign land but God was with him. While Joseph was a slave in the land of Egypt, it seemed as if everything and everyone was against him, but he held on to his dream. Joseph was accused of rape, cast into prison for a crime he didn't commit. God showed him the future through a dream. What dream has God given you?

When you are in the right place in the right timing of God, the blessing will somehow find its way to you. When you are in the right city, the right marriage, on the right job, the blessing will find you. Joseph said, to his brothers, *"do not be afraid, for I am in the place of God?"* But as for you, you meant evil, but God meant it for good, in order to bring it about as it is this day to save many people alive. Genesis 50:19-20.

With every dream or vision comes opposition. In this life there will be times that it will seem as if everything is against you, there will be battle after battle. If you don't see the manifestation of God's hand, just trust his plan."

So it was when his master heard the words which his wife spoke to him saying, your servant did to me after this manner, that his anger was aroused and put him in the prison a place where the King's prisoners were confined and he was there in prison but the Lord was with Joseph and showed him mercy and gave him favor in the sight of the keeper of the prison and the keeper of the prison committed to Joseph's hand all the prisoners who were in the prison whatever they did there it was his doing the keeper of the prison did not look into anything that was under his hand. Genesis 39:19.

In spite of all, Joseph was going through and where he was in his life, he held on to faith and he kept focus on the dream. He knew that his dream would someday happen. *"In hope of eternal life which God that cannot lie promised before the world began."* Titus 1:2. God promises will come to pass. *Whatever he promised he will manifest not a word failed of any good thing which the Lord has spoken to the house of Israel, all came to pass."* Joshua 24:45 NKJV.

I would like to say to the body of Christ. There is nothing wrong with asking the Lord why. God has the answer to your why. I believe if, you ask the Lord in humility, and reverently; He will explain to you why. God is not going to punish you for asking Him why.

I believe if you knew the reason why it happened, no doubt you would know how to move forward to your destiny, this will bring equilibrium to any adversity. We must learn to give God thanks in everything in this life and you may not have what you want to have but continue to give God thanks anyway!

Apostle Paul is a historian that we can look to as one pressing toward his destiny, regardless of what he was going through. *"Are they ministers of Christ? I speak as a fool, I am more, in labours, more abundant in stripes, above measure, in prisons more frequently in deaths oft. From the Jews, 5 times I received five stripes minus one. Three times I was beaten with rods; once I was stoned; three times I was shipwreck; a night and day I have been in the deep: in journeys often: in perils of waters, in perils of robbers, in perils of my own countrymen, in perils of the Gentiles. In perils in the city, in perils in the wilderness, in perils in the sea, in perils among false brethren: in weariness and toil, in sleeplessness often, in hungry and thirst, in fastings often, in cold and nakedness besides the other things, what comes upon me daily : my concern for all the churches. Who is weak and I am not weak? Who is made to stumble, and I do not burn with indignation? If I must boast, I will boast in the things which concern my infirmity. The God and Father of our Lord Jesus Christ, who is blessed forever, knows that I am not lying."* II Corinthians 11:23 NKJV.

I myself must keep pressing regardless of all the impossibilities that I am facing. I could complain right now about many things. If I did complain, I would only entertain self-pity. Therefore, I would rather give thanks, that things are as well as they are. Complaining will not help the situation. According to the will of God, it is the will of God to give thanks! A person who complains is a very selfish person.

I don't complain about the AVM, neither do I complain about spending 57 days in the hospital, or about the medical bills that exceeded half of a million dollars. I don't complain about the church members who walked away from the ministry. They thought it was all over for me and the church, because of the brain aneurysm. They thought I would never return to the pulpit. Matter of fact, the word was out in the Christian community that I had died.

I was released from the hospital to go home on a walker. Every day for about two months, I had to shower by siting in a chair. I was also diagnosed with vertigo. Dizziness is one of the most common symptoms, along with nausea or vomiting or both, spinning of the room and blurred vision are connected with it. I was unable to drive for nine months due to the doctor's orders. For nine months, Lady Holly had to do all the driving. When the doctor gave me the green light to drive; I did and totaled two vehicles. With each accident, I walked away without a scratch.

One day my wife wanted me to go shopping with her. at the Oak Park Mall. I was on a walker. As I went inside, the floor seemed to vibrate. The shelves looked as if they were closing in on me. I turned around and went back to my vehicle. It was about a year before I could go back to any of the department or grocery stores. I asked my doctor about this, and the doctor said that my brain was still shrinking from the AVM.

Though others may have turned and walked away, my wife was right by my side; spending nights with me while in the hospital. She was also hurting because of the things I was going through. There were times I would turn my head from her, so that she wouldn't see me cry because of the pain that I felt. I've experienced a lot of dark, dark, days.

I once heard Bishop T. D. Jakes say, "if you ever become helpless in anyway make sure you have plenty of good health insurance, because people will walk away from your side." I know that a grown man is not supposed to cry. For me, crying at times would be a relief. This was not to say that I didn't have any faith.

Job experienced a trial season where his relatives, acquaintances, and friends isolated themselves from him because he had experienced a great fall. It is funny how people don't want to have anything to do with you, when it appears that you are down and out, and it seems as if you're never going to get back on your feet. I know you're saying; "I know exactly what that feels like." If you haven't experienced it, you really don't know, nor can you really say what it feels like.

"And the Lord restored Job's losses when he prayed for his friends; indeed the Lord gave Job twice as much as he had before. Then all his brothers and his sisters in all those that had been his acquaintances before came to

him and ate food with him in his house; and they consoled him and conformed him for all the adversary that the Lord had brought upon him. Each gave him a piece of silver and each a ring of gold. Now the Lord blessed the latter days of Job more than his beginning." Job 42: 10-12.

How did Satan get to Job, when there was a hedge around him? The Bible teaches that if there is an opening in the hedge or if the hedge is down, the enemy will come in. *"If there be a breach in the hedge the serpent will bite him."* Ecclesiastes, 10:8. The Lord was not testing Job, because He already knew the outcome of Job.

There are those who believe that sickness and disease come from God to teach you something or to give you some type of message. God is a good God. I don't believe that at all. The last time I read the bible, it said that Jesus took our infirmities and bore all sickness. Therefore, God cannot be associated with sickness nor disease. Another scripture says, *"if you then being evil know how to give good gifts to your children, how much more will your Father in heaven give good things to those who ask Him."* Matthew 7:11. God loves you and I, so why would he put sickness on us.

I would like to ask you some questions; Do you have children? Do you love your children? Have they disappointed you at times? Would you put cancer or some other incurable disease on them to teach them something or to give them a message? Sickness and disease are evil. Let no one say when he is tempted, *"I am tempted by God for God cannot be tempted by evil nor does he Himself tempted anyone."* James 1:13 NKJV.

Chapter 3
Close the Door

The thief does not come except to steal and to kill and to destroy I have come that they may have life and that they may have it more abundantly." John 10:10 NKJV. Jesus lets us know that the devil only has a three-fold purpose and they are to kill, to steal and destroy. You must keep the door closed spiritually, mentally, emotionally, physically, and financially.

If there are any doors or cracks that or open, the devil is coming with his three-fold purpose to try and take you out. The devil can only take you out if the door is open. *"Neither give place to the devil."* Ephesian 4:27. Another translation says to give no occupancy to the devil. *"Be sober be vigilant; because your adversary the devil, as a roaring lion, walketh, about seeking whom he may devour,* I Peter 5:5. The enemy is coming to check and see if all your doors are closed and locked. He can only devour those whose doors are opened.

What Peter is saying not to think like a person that is intoxicated. A person who is intoxicated doesn't think soberly. Neither will he make the best choices. If there is a crack that the enemy can come through; guess what? He's coming! The Lord has designed it so that the enemy just can't come in to you without you surrendering your will.

Again, he can only get in if there is an opening. You may not be aware of any openings. This is why you must constantly ask the Holy Spirit to reveal certain things to you. Ignorance fuels flames for the devil's purpose. Just because you are unaware of an opening, does not mean that you are excused from its reaping. God nor Satan, will not go against your will. *"Behold I stand at the door and knock; If any man hear my voice, and open the door, "I will come into him and sup with him and he with me."* Revelation 3:20. If you want God to come in, you have to open the door.

We live in a fallen world because of Adam's transgression. Therefore, we must have knowledge concerning the laws that governs the physical and spiritual world. The body of Christ only view laws from a spiritual side and ignore the natural side. Remember there is a God side, and a man side. If you are going to be successful in this life, you must understand the principals of both sides and how they function.

I hear many believers binding and loosing things here in the earth, and are not seeing results of their declarations. The reason why they are not seeing results is because they don't have an understanding of principles. *"And I will give unto thee the keys of the kingdom of heaven; and whatsoever thou, shalt bind on earth shall be bound in heaven, and whatsoever thou shall loose on earth shall be loosed in heaven."* Matthew 16:19. The keys that Jesus was referring to are the authority and principles that governs the physical and spiritual world. If you have knowledge and understanding of the physical and spiritual laws, then you are able to bind and loose.

My mother passed away at the age of 45. It was a premature death. She didn't give much attention to the natural process for her healing. The doctor recommended a bone marrow transplant. This would have reduced the leukemia disease to zero. She believed in divine healing. My uncle Bobby was a bone match for her. The manifestation of her healing would have come through the natural process of the transplant operation. This was God's way of healing her. I believe the reason why the Body of Christ pursues the spiritual side of things is that 100% of the time the physical or natural requires discipline and work.

The people of God are looking for a quick fix to every problem. They want some abracadabra; hocus pocus, trick for their problems. In other words, they want something instantaneous. Listen to me closely; this is not magic and this is not luck! God has designed a system for all to follow in order to get results. If we live by principles and faith, we will see the miracle.

It is not the will of God that we live from miracle to miracle. Rather, we should live from principal to principal. God is not going to do what you are capable of doing. He will only do what you are unable to do.

You must attack every problem with a strategic plan. Remember your plan will require work. You will not wish some things away. If you do not plan, you've planned to fail.

For example if you want to lose weight by dieting, not only do you pray about it (spiritually) you must also activate a plan (naturally). *"For as the body without the spirit is dead, so faith without works is dead also."* James 2:26. I believe that Jesus was in great health! He worked as a carpenter. He walked just about everywhere he went. He was very active and physically fit. He ate healthy and he made sure he rested properly. He did those things that are needed in the natural realm.

Jesus was theoanthropos. In the Greek, this means He was fully God and fully man. He was God manifested in the flesh. He is the Son of God as well as the son of man. He was both human and divine. Jesus got hungry as a man, he got thirsty as a man, he prayed as a man, he walked on water as a man, and He was even tempted as a man. *"For we have a high priest which cannot be touched with the feelings of our infirmities but in all points tempted like as we are yet without sin."* Hebrews 4:15. He knows what you are going through. Jesus as a man felt what you feel.

The average person doesn't want to visit the doctor for the fear of what the doctor may discover. If you are planning to do the Lord's work, you really need to make sure you are healthy. If you discover sickness in its early stages, chances are, you will conquer the battle. The Bible is a book of living principles that we are to obey to get the results we are looking for. In obeying these principles, it closes the door to any evil that will try to come in. I was talking with a guy who said that it's ok for us to eat anything as long as we bless our food by saying grace as we pray over it. *"For every creature of God is good and nothing to be refused, if it be received with thanksgiving; For it is sanctified, by the word and prayer."* I Timothy 4:4-5. Yes, you can eat what you please. Remember, if it's not done in moderation you will have to pay a price for eating those things.

Wisdom is the principal thing; "therefore get wisdom; and in all thy getting get understanding." Proverbs 4:7.
There are some that believe if you go to a doctor you don't have any faith, or you're not trusting God. *"But of him are in Christ Jesus, who of God is made unto us wisdom and righteousness, and sanctification, and redemption."* 1 Corinthians 1:30. Jesus was made wisdom unto us; I believe that it is a wise man that will get examined by a doctor. The spirit of wisdom will tell you what you should eat and what time you should not eat. The spirit of wisdom will tell you to drink more water Instead of tea or soda. These beverages will contribute to dehydration. The spirit of wisdom will tell

you to eat more fruit, salad and vegetables. God's spirit will inform us of how and what to consume in moderation. In addition, wisdom will advise you on the type of diet that is best for you. Just because others are doing a great program doesn't mean it's the right one for you.

If you are going down the highway the wrong way, you are bound to have an accident. I had an accident when I had the AVM of the brain. I thank God I'm still alive and that the grace of God has given me another chance to fulfill the will of God for my life. Those who are spiritual minded, need to become educated with the human body and its function. We are living in times that men are spraying our vegetation to protect them from insects with different pesticides. Water treatment plants are trying to clean our drinking water with unsafe chemicals. The different chemicals are working against the human body. Did you know many medications that people are indulging in have serious side effects?

There are over 100,000 people dying each year in the United States from the side-effects of medicine. A lot of sickness is linked to food, vaccinations, medications and in the water that we drink causing aluminum in the brain. As a result there's an increase in Alzheimer's, dementia, autism, attention deficit hyperactivity disorder (ADHD), Down's syndrome, bipolar and other diseases. I believe these are some of the reasons for the increase of these diseases. When I was growing up as a kid, I never heard of many of these diseases. When a door is open in any area that will give trouble an entry, the Holy Spirit can reveal to you where the door is open in your life. You may not have any clue that a door is open.

Nothing just happens. If something occurs, there is a reason why it happened. If there is any kind of opening that will allow different, things to come in your life you can't blame God for this. *"As the bird by wondering, as the swallow by flying, so the curse cause less, shall not come."* Proverbs 26:2. The curse is still operating in the world today. As a believer in Jesus Christ, we are redeemed from the curse. *"Christ has redeemed us from the curse of the law having become a curse for us as it is written cursed is everyone who hangs on a tree that the blessing of Abraham might come upon the Gentiles in Christ Jesus that we might receive the promise of the spirit through faith."* Galatians 3:13-14 NKJV.

Yes, we are redeemed from the curse, but we must renew our minds to the Word of God so that we will not make our own decisions. When the wrong choices are made, you open the door to evil things. *"I call heaven and earth to record this day against you, that I have set before you life and death blessings and cursing: therefore choose life that both thou and thy seed may live."* Deuteronomy 30:19. Your choices and your decisions will have an impact on your family. In the book of Deuteronomy, Moses tells the second generation of Israel to choose life.

A crisis is something that happens that you have no control over. I know you are thinking only if I can return to that place and correct all the bad. If I had another chance, I would do things differently. Only if I knew then what I know now my choices would be different, but the excuses of woulda, coulda, shoulda cannot correct the past. What is done is done. It is what it is!

The people of New Orleans faced a crisis when Hurricane Katrina hit the city. The people in the city had no control over what happened in New Orleans; buildings and cars were underwater, there was loss of life, and families were separated all across the country as a result. The nation watched the news in horror and disbelief of the terrible things that happened in that city. It was hard to believe that such things were occurring right before our very eyes in the United States of America. Following the hurricane aftermath, those that escaped from the city of New Orleans were called refugees.

New Orleans has made a comeback. The New Orleans Saints NFL football team won a Super Bowl championship. There are buildings and businesses opening and under construction. Just as New Orleans has made a comeback after Hurricane Katrina, you and I can make a comeback after a fall. You must trouble proof your life by staying in the presence of God and applying his word to your life daily.

None of us are exempt from trouble and tribulation. We live in this fallen world and therefore trouble, trials and tribulation comes with the package. *"These things I have spoken unto you, that in me ye might have peace." "In the world ye shall have tribulation; but be of good cheer, I have overcome the world."* John 16:33.

Jesus said in this life we will have tribulation. Tribulation means severe afflictions and stresses, and trouble in this life that proceeds from persecution. There is no way around this. Tribulation comes to everyone. Everyone will have his or her evil day. *Therefore take up the whole armor of God that you may be able to withstand in the evil day and having done all, to stand; stand therefore having girded your waist with truth having put on the breastplate of righteousness."* Ephesians 6:13-14 NKJV. An evil day is a season of tribulation.

Again there is no way around it, everyone will experience an evil day. *"Therefore whoever here's the things of mine and do them I will like in him to a wise man who built his house on the rock, and the rain descended and the floods came and the wind blew and beat on that house and it did not fall for it was founded on the rock but everyone who hear these things of mine and does not do them will be like a foolish man who built his house on this thing and the rain descended the floods came and the winds blew and beat on that house and it fell. And great was its fall."* Matthew 7: 24-27 NKJV. Notice Jesus did not say if the rain comes, or if the winds blow, or if it floods, but he said when the rain comes, when the wind blows, and when the floods come. Jesus was saying not if it happens but when it happens.

In this life, the storm is going to come but you will not crumble if you are established on the rock, which is the revelation of God's word. *"Therefore my brethren; count it all joy when you fall into divers temptations."* James 1:2. The reason why James said count it all joy is because God has already made a way for you to come out of it. Remember, in every temptation there is also a way of an escape. Again noticed this; James didn't say count it all joy if you fall. However when you fall into divers temptations; God will turn it around for you and causes it to help develop you. Then you may learn from it, *knowing this, the trying of your faith worketh patience. But let patience have her perfect work that you may be perfect mature an entire wanting nothing.* James 1:4. Therefore, all of us need to prepare for the evil day. The evil day is not the last days. The evil day is the season of tribulation, testing, and trials.

When people ask the question why did this happen to me? They do so with an attitude of anger and bitterness. Complaining is not going to fix anything, complaining will get you know where. *"For a just man falls seven times and rises up again."* Proverbs 24:16.

Maurice Williams

Chapter 4
Stress or Rest?

In this chapter, I talk about several things that will bring on stress. As a believer, your body was not designed to take on stress. You have the Holy Spirit of God living on the inside of you, to lead and guide you. *"And lead us not into temptation, but deliver us from evil; for thine is the kingdom, and power, and the glory, forever, amen."* Matthew 6:13.

The Holy Spirit will never lead you where His power cannot keep you. Now it is up to you, to choose either *stress or rest*. Rest is always connected to faith. If you don't have peace and you are not at rest, you're not in the will of God. The author gives us an oxymoron, in the fourth chapter of the book of Hebrews. He tells us to work to rest! How do we work to rest? By trusting in God's word and believing what it takes to conceive the promise. When the promise is conceived in our hearts, then we rest and wait for the manifestation. There is nothing else left to do. *"Let us labor therefore to enter into that rest, lest any man falleth after the same example of unbelief."* Hebrews 4:1. As we live by faith, we rest in the words of Jesus. Everything that you will ever need or desire was completed in Jesus on the cross of Calvary.

If you believe in what Jesus has said, you can't help but to rest. We do not bring to pass anything in our own strength. *"Except the Lord build the house they labor in vain that build it: except the Lord keep the city, the watchman waketh but in vain. It is vain for you to rise up early to sit up late to eat the bread of Sorrows, for so he giveth his beloved sleep."* Psalms 127:1-2.

The Lord will give us sweet sleep. While it may be storming in our lives. *"and they sent the multitudes away they took him even as he was in the ship and there were also with him other little ships and there arose a great Storm of wind and the waves beat into the ship so that it was now full. And he was in the hinder part of the ship asleep on a pillow and they awake him master carest, not that we perish?"* Mark 4: 36-38.

Sometimes we are often stressed by trying to help God bring the promise to pass. Other times we experience stress when we try to master several things at the same time, being analytical, outside the will and the perfect timing of God. Remember this, if it's not His will; it will become your bill. When we rest God goes to work and brings to pass all that was finished in Jesus for you and I.

Whatever we set our minds to do, we must make sure that the blessing of God is with us. "The blessing of the Lord, it maketh, rich and he added no sorrow with it." Proverbs 10:22. When you receive the blessing and you are trusting God, He will always lead you into battles that you don't have to fight. The battles are not yours but God's, and you will rest and not stress. Now thanks be to

God who always leads us into triumph in Christ." II Corinthians 2:14.

"This know also, that in the last days perilous times shall come" II Timothy 3:1. Paul wrote an epistle to his son in the gospel, whose name was Timothy. This letter was one of the last of the three Pastoral Epistles that was written to both Titus and Timothy. Another translation of that verse says; *"This know also that in the last days stressful times shall come."* Everywhere you turn, people are stressed. Question, is a little stress good for you? No, not at all. Stress is an attribute, of the spirit of fear. *"For God has not given us the Spirit of fear; but of power and of love, and of a sound mind. "* II Timothy 1:7. Stress is birth out of fear; it manifests itself in toxic thoughts, worry, depression, acceleration of aging, nervousness, restlessness, weight loss, and pre-mature gray hairs. We will talk more about stress and rest throughout this chapter.

The number one reason people stress is over finances. *"No man can serve two masters; for either he will hate the one, and love the other; or else he will hold to the one, and despise the other."* *Ye cannot serve God and mamon."* Matthew 6:24. Mammon was the god of the Philistines. Mammon is defined as the god of interest, or the money system of debt. Then, Goliath the champion of the Philistines, who's name also means debt. He was defeated by a little shepherd boy named David.

"So David prevailed over the Philistines with a sling and with a stone, and smote the Philistine, and slew him; but there was no sword in the hand of David." Therefore, David ran and stood upon the Philistine, and took his sword, and drew it out of the sheath thereof, and slew him, and cut off his head therewith. And when the Philistines, saw there champion was dead, they fled."
I Samuel 17:50-51.

People today are overwhelmed with debt. They are stressing, and struggling with debt. Purchasing things on credit and paying for them later seems to be the only way to the American dream. Actually, this is the world's system of operation. In most cases, it takes thirty years to pay off a mortgage. It now takes years to pay off credit card debt, if you're paying only the monthly minimum. Most families need five to seven years to pay off a new car.

If you are in deep financial debt and can't pay what you owe; the system says the easy way out is to file bankruptcy and get out of it. Most people find themselves right back into debt because of poor management of their finances and do not learn from their mistakes. The number one reason couple's divorce is because of debt. Churches are in debt. The people of God are in debt and cannot finance God's agenda
.

Here are some reasons why people go into debt: divorce, loss of job, health issues, a recession, student loans, or some other unforeseen mishap. God will reveal a strategic plan to get out of debt. There's a question that's been asked over the years; the question, is borrowing a sin? The Bible clearly says " *owe no man anything but love one another but he that loveth another have fulfilled the law* Romans 13 8. If borrowing is a sin, then lending has to be a sin. Moses tells the nation of Israel "*and thou shalt lend unto many nations and thou shall not borrow." Deuteronomy 28:12. Another scripture reading says, *Elijah told the widow woman go borrow the vessels abroad of all thy neighbor's even empty vessels borrow not a few." II Kings 4:3.

Stress can come upon you because of a lack of patience. People want things right now, they can't seem to wait. People want things now even if they have to charge to get them. There will always be a price to pay for not waiting, because of the mammon.

Jesus said, "*in patience possess ye your soul." Luke 21:9. We know the soul is the mind, will, emotions, intellect, and imagination. If you are patient in this realm, you will become more like Jesus. Patience is not putting up with something, neither is it the tolerance of things, but rather the endurance of remaining the same in or out of tribulation. Stress is unseen pressure that weighs on your emotions.
This pressure quietly drapes you without you ever knowing it has placed a blanket around you.

God gave your emotions to you. If you don't guard your mind, stress will oppress your emotions. Once it oppresses your emotions, it can affect you physically producing sickness and disease.

There have been members of our church who went to visit their doctor because they were not feeling well. The doctor examined them, and all vitals were normal. The reason why their test results came back normal was that their symptoms were related to stress. Stress affects people in different ways. Some people sleep, others don't get enough sleep at all. Stress can be very silent, but it speaks loudly.

Strive to abide in the will of God. Did you know that the safest place in a hurricane is right smack dab in the middle of the eye? If you're in the middle of God's will, you are safe. No matter how bad the storm is around you, there will be protection, prosperity, provisions, and peace.

Are you an anxious individual? Do you have a problem with anxiety? Don't get ahead of God. Allow him to lead you in His perfect will, and timing. God has an appointed time for your promise to manifest. Wait for God. *"Be anxious for nothing, but in everything by prayer and supplications, with thanksgiving, let your request be made known to God."* Philippians 4:6. If what you are believing God for has not manifested; there are reasons for the delay. Remember, a delay is not a denial.

If there is a delay, there are reasons why! Such as, God may be waiting for you to mature. Maybe God is orchestrating things and putting them in alignment, or God is ministering to every heart that is involved to bring about the manifestation. Every delay is in your favor! Again, a delay is not a denial.

If you can't wait for God to manifest the promise, your emotions will be stressed from worrying. Worry is meditation of negative thought; *"Finally, brethren, whatsoever things are true, whatsoever things are honest, whatsoever things are just, whatsoever things are pure, whatsoever things are lovely, whatsoever things are of good report; if there be any virtue if there be any praise, think on these things."* Philippians 4:8.

Worrying about things will not change any facts, because it will stress you out. Jesus said *"which of you by worrying can add one cubit to his stature?"* Matthew 6:27 NKJ. You can't change anything by worrying. Worry comes from the spirit of fear. It may be that you're analytical. You would like to know when, why, and how God is going to bring the promise to pass.

Your delay of manifestation is based on your maturity, and growth in the grace of God. *"Now I say, that the heir as long as he is a child differeth, nothing from a servant, though he be Lord of all: but is under tutors and governors until the time appointed of the Father."*

Galatians 4:1-2. I would like to ask you a question. Do you think you're able to handle the manifestation or should I ask can you stand to be blessed? Many times people say I am waiting on the Lord, but really, the Lord is waiting on you. *"And behold the word of the Lord came unto him saying this shall not be thine heir; but he that shall come forth out of thine own bowels shall be thine heir."* Genesis 15: 4.

God told Abram he would have a Son. For Abram and Sarai, this process of the supernatural manifestation was taking too long. Sarai came up with a plan to try to help God bring this promise to pass. *"So Sarai said to Abram; "See now the Lord has restrained me from bearing children. Please go in to my maid; perhaps I shall obtain children by her." And Abram heeded the voice of Sarai. Then Sarai, Abram ' s wife took Hager her maid, the Egyptian, and gave her to her husband Abram to be his wife, after Abram had dwelt ten years in the land of Canaan. So he went in to Hagar, and she conceived. And when she saw that she had conceived, her mistress became despised in her eyes."* Genesis 16: 2-4. God doesn't need your help. He doesn't need my help. God is help all by himself.*" God is our refuge and strength a very present help in trouble."* Psalms 46:1. Abram and Sarai couldn't wait for God to manifest the supernatural as a result they gave birth to Ishmael.

Another way you can bring on stress is by trying to master several things at the same time. You may be called to do something, but you are not called to do everything. My mission is to tell the body of Christ not to get overwhelmed by trying to master everything. In my experience, I would say yes to everyone. I would try to make every invitation. I thought I was invincible but I was really becoming vulnerable by saying yes to everyone and everything. Because I am a minister, I would say yes.

We are living in the days of swift communication. Almost everything today is fast-paced and the only thing that travels slowly is good news. Did you know that bad news travels fast? If something bad, happens in the world? Within a very short amount of time, bad news will air on CNN, the Internet or some other news broadcast. The communication of the Internet, texting, cell phones, fax machines, email, Facebook, Instagram and Twitter; each communication delivers the message speedily. Satan is the prince and the power of the air. One definition for the word *air* is translated, *communication*. Satan is using these different forms of communication to spread his message. I believe that these forms of communications along with technology should also be used to spread the *good news* of the gospel.

I witnessed how swift everything moves personally. On a trip, we landed in the Atlanta Airport. We began walking to baggage claim. I noticed that everyone was walking so fast we were being passed quickly. I asked myself, why is everyone walking so fast? They were not walking fast; we were walking slowly! I believe that they were walking the pace of the city. I believe that the City of Atlanta is faster paced than Kansas City where I am from. I was walking the pace of Kansas City in the Atlanta Airport! Now, I believe that there are some cities faster-paced than others. Those cities also have more stress in them. *"Be anxious for nothing; but in everything by prayer and supplication with thanksgiving let your request be made known unto God."* Philippians 4:6 NKJV.

If you do not rest, you will stress. *"And on the seventh day God ended his work. Which he had done, and He rested on the seventh day from all His work which he had done."* Genesis 2:2 NKJV God did not rest because He was tired, He rested because He was finished. All things are finished for us this is why we should rest. *"When Jesus therefore had received the vinegar, he said it is finished: and he bowed his head and gave up the ghost."* John19:30. If you are overworked and you're not getting enough rest you're going to stress. I believe that there are times that you need to drop everything, step back, and get some rest. I always say if you don't come apart, you will come a part. *"And he said unto them, come ye yourselves apart into a desert place, and rest a while."* Mark 6:31. You may be working yourself and saying I can't take a vacation I've got so much to do. I'm too busy if I don't do it; then it won't get done. Listen to me. Take some time for yourself and take a vacation. Not taking time away was a downfall for me. There were times I didn't take a vacation. When you take a vacation, I guarantee you the work will be there when you return. Don't ever think that if you don't do it; it will not get done. If I had died, the church that I pastor would have moved forward without me.

Employers, corporations, and companies know if they give their employees a vacation, they will return to work refreshed. When people take on obligations that God didn't tell them to accept, it will ultimately lead to stress. If you try to make things happen or bring to pass your prayers in your own ability and by trying to give God a helping hand. You will become full of stress. This happens when you can't wait for God. *"Wait on the Lord be of good courage and he shall strengthen thine heart wait I say on the Lord."* Psalms 27 14.

Again, being analytical is when you must know every detail on how God is going to come through for you or how he's going to deliver you. I know you are saying you're in faith, but you really don't know that you are in fear. This is pressure applied to your emotions. Pressure is a strain, or a stress, that weighs on you. It is pressure applied to the emotions. You really don't know what you are made of until pressure is applied. When pressure is applied to your emotions, whatever is deeply seated in your heart will eventually surface by coming out of your mouth.

We are living in a time where people want to skip over process to obtain everything now. People want whatever they want right now without having to go through any process at all to get it. I don't know if you have noticed it or not, but people are speeding more than ever before. Do you speed when you drive? If you speed when you drive, this may be an indication that you are stressed. You must find a way to rest in the words of Jesus. I know you want to ask the question; how do we not stress in a stressful society? I'm giving you some tips on how not to stress and how to close all doors that may be open to stress. Stress is also a silent killer if it is not detected it will lead to different diseases.*" and let the peace of God rule in your hearts to the which also you are called in one body and be thankful. "* Colossians 3: 15 NKJV.

If your soul is not at peace with your decision, your decision is not the right decision. If it's not the correct decision, your spirit will warn you before you make the wrong decision. Your peace should always be still. Remember, your peace should never fluctuate.

Chapter 5
Your History is not Your Destiny

Everyone can remember their history. History is who you are from the past, and what your past says about you. Everyone has a past. Your history may be either good or bad.

Let's walk down memory lane. There are things that you and I have done that were totally against the will of God. Once you confess Jesus, your history is washed away. You become a new species of being that has never existed before, or a new creation. Therefore, it is impossible for you to have any history. *Therefore, if any man be in Christ he is a new creature. Old things are passed away; Behold all things are become new."* II Corinthians 5:17

There is a man in the Bible whose name was Jacob, his name means cheater, deceiver, supplanter, and catcher. He had plenty of history, but God changed his name from Jacob to Israel. Israel means Prince of God. *"Then Jacob was left alone, and a man wrestled with him until the breaking of day. Now, when he saw that he did not prevail against him, he touched the socket of his hip, and the socket of Jacob's hip was out of joint as he wraps it with him and he said, let me go for the day breaks, but he said I will not let you go unless you bless me, so he said to him what is your name? He said Jacob, and he said your name shall no longer be called Jacob but Israel, for you have struggled with God and with men and have prevailed." Genesis 24:28* NKJV.

God has purposed you for destiny before the foundation of the world. If you have experienced a fall, know this that God still has a plan for you to make it to your destiny. You are not defined by where you are, or where you have been or who they say you are. God will use the good and the bad that happens in your life to bring you to destiny. *"The steps of a good man are ordered by the Lord; and he delighted in his way, though he fall, he shall not be utterly cast down; for the Lord upholds him with His hand."* Psalms 37: 23-24.

People will never allow you to be free from your past. Since you are moving towards destiny, God is all that matters, not people. People will always remember your history, but not God. I found out you can't stop people from thinking what they want to think about you. GOD forgives and He chooses to forget. *"For I will be merciful to their sins and their iniquities, will I remember no more."* Hebrews 8:12. God has a remedy for your history, also for your present and future. It is the blood of Jesus. *"If we confess our sins, he is faithful and just to forgive us our sins, and to cleanse us from all unrighteousness."* I John 1:9. If you are forgiven, you no longer have any history, the blood of Jesus gives you the position of righteousness in God. The grace of God is an empowerment given to you to arrive at your destiny. If your fall is not dealt with from a spiritual perspective, you will have lingering questions on your mind, for instance;

- o   Will I ever be used by God again?
- o   Will I ever open another business,
- o   Will I ever get married again?
- o   Did I miss my season?
- o   Will I get another chance?

There is another man in the Bible whose name is Sampson. He fell into sin and lost his anointing. He never forgot the purpose for which he was born. Sampson was anointed to be a Judge, a ruler over the people of Israel. His purpose was to deliver the people of God from the oppression of the Philistines. Sampson lost his anointing when the Philistines cut his hair.

"But the Philistines took him, and put out his eyes, and brought him down to Gaza and bound him with fetters and brass; and he did grind in the prison house." Judges 16:21. Sin brought him so low that he was grinding at the mill in the prison house of the enemy.

The great judge has now become a slave. This is what sin does to you; it makes you its slave. Sin will always take you farther than you want to go. *"However the hair of his head began to grow again after it had been shaven."* Judges 16:22.

Sampson is a type of Christ. Sampson destroyed more Philistines in his death than in his life. Likewise, Jesus defeated the host of hell in his death than in His life. *"And having spoiled principalities and powers he made a shew of them openly, triumphing over them in it."* Colossians 2:15.

Another man in the Bible by the name of Jonah made a major mistake, but he fulfilled the purpose of God that was on his life. You may have made some major mistakes but the purpose of God is still burning on the inside of you. What I'm trying to say is God has not changed his mind concerning his purpose for you.

"Now the word of the Lord came unto Jonah the son of Amittai, saying. Arise go to Nineveh that great city, and cry against it; for their wickedness is come up before me, but Jonah rose up to flee unto Tarshish, from the presence of; the Lord, and went down to Joppa: And he found a ship going to Tarshish; So he paid the fare thereof and went down to it to go with them unto Tarshish from the presence of the Lord." Jonah 1:1-3. If you go in the opposite direction and do things on your own, you will end up paying for the trip. God is not going to pay for what he has not sanctioned. Notice Jonah paid his own way to Tarshish, because he didn't want to go to Nineveh. He went the other way. Jonah's disobedience to the voice of God was the reason he ended up in the belly of the whale. I believe Jonah died in the whale's belly. *"For as Jonah was three days and three nights in the whales belly so shall the Son of man be three days and three nights in the heart of the earth."*

Matthew 12:40. Before he died, he began to pray to God. *"And the Lord spake unto the fish and it vomit out Jonah upon the dry land."* Jonah 2:10. God did not change his plan because of Jonah ' s disobedience. Jonah shows us that he is an example of one whom God did not change his mind concerning His purpose and plan. Jonah messed up big time! But the bible says that the word of the Lord came to Jonah the second time. *"Arise, go unto Nineveh that great city, and preach unto it the preaching that I bid thee."* Jonah 3:2. Notice it was the same word, with the same purpose. Jonah's history was not his destiny.

Remember the apostle Peter; he also messed up. Peter was the disciple that received a revelation from the Almighty God, that Jesus was the Christ, the Son of the living God. During the last Passover supper, Jesus told His disciples that one of them would betray him and another would deny him. Peter said although others may leave you I am willing to go to prison with you even die for you and he said, *"I tell thee Peter the cock shall not crow this day before that thou shalt thrice deny that thou knowest me."* Luke 22:34.

Later that evening the temple guards went to the Garden of Gethsemane to arrest Jesus. Peter saw the power of the words of Jesus when he said *"I am he"* John 18:5 and the temple guards fell to the ground. Peter thought within himself that this was his chance to prove that he was right and Jesus was wrong." *Then Simon Peter having a sword drew it, and smote the high priest's servant and cut off his right ear. The servants name was Malchus."* John 18:10.

"Then said Jesus unto Peter put up thy sword into the sheath: the cup which my Father hath given me shall I not drink it." John 18: 11. When Jesus submitted to the priests, elders, the band of captains and officers, which came to arrest him; Peter and all the disciples fled. The disciples knew that anyone claiming to be king would be sentenced to death along with his entire cabinet, because this was considered treason. *"And they all forsook him and fled."* Mark 14:50.

Three witnesses confronted Peter concerning his association with Jesus. Each time Peter was questioned, he denied ever knowing Jesus. The temple guards would have arrested Peter, but they didn't because he had previously cursed when he was confronted. They knew that anyone who cursed like Peter did could not have been associated with Jesus. *"And the Lord turned and looked upon Peter and Peter remembered the word of the Lord, how he said unto him, before the cock crow, thou shalt deny me thrice." And Peter went out and wept bitterly."* Luke 22:61-62. After the resurrection, the angle appeared to the women and said, *"Ye seek Jesus of Nazareth which was crucified: He is risen; He is not here; Behold the place where they laid him. But go your way; tell his disciples and Peter, that he goeth, before*

*you into Galilee. There shall ye see Him, as he said unto
you. "* Mark 16:6-7.

The reason the angel said tell His disciples and Peter is
because Peter had experienced a fall. He was carrying
guilt, shame, and condemnation. Peter walked away
from the ministry and went back to doing what he knew
best. Peter said I have failed the Lord Jesus; I have
messed up, what is the use in continuing in ministry.
*"This is now the third time that Jesus showed Himself to
His disciples. After that, He was risen from the dead.
"So when they had dined, Jesus saith to Simon
Peter, Simon son of Jonas, lovest (agape) thou me more
than these? He saith unto Him yea Lord; thou knoweth
that I love (phileo) these. Feed my lambs. "* John 21:15.

Agape is the God kind of love. It means to love
unconditionally; ardently; supremely; and also perfectly.
Phileo also means to like; to be fond of; to have love for
a brother. *"He saith to him again the second
time, Simon, Son of Jonas lovest* (agape) *thou me? He
saith unto him, feed my sheep. He saith unto him the
third time, Simon son of Jonas lovest (phileo) thou me?
Peter was grieved because He said unto Him, Lord thou
knowest all things: thou knowest that I love* (agape) *thee.
Jesus said unto him, feed my sheep. "* John 21:14-17.
Peter was being very cautious of what he was about to
say. He thought about it carefully, this time, thinking
before he spoke. He didn't want to make the same
mistake twice. Jesus kept asking Peter do you love me? I

believe that Jesus was trying to get a true confession out of him. Jesus wasn't asking the questions to convict him, or condemn him. He asked the questions to affirm him back into the ministry. Jesus knew that Peter loved him. He wanted Peter to be comfortable saying it. In saying it, it will become a reality. This would also cancel out Peter's three previous denials. Peter's confession helped to release the guilt and shame. God still used Peter, and brought him into destiny, fulfilling the plan of God. If Peter can cut a man's ear off, deny Jesus, curse, and quit the ministry, surely there is hope for you! I'm going to go one-step beyond that. God used three murders (Moses, David, Paul) to fulfill His plan. We know that our history is not our destiny.

There are many others in the Bible I could have mentioned concerning their history. God shows us both sides of man. God shows his potential, purpose achievements and successes; and his failures and flaws.. This is why I know God influenced man by His Spirit to write the Bible. Man would never expose himself by writing about his sins. God shows both sides of men in the Bible. He also shows us his mercy and grace.

One thing I like about the grace of God, it covers you, and it can cause all your mistakes to prosper. This is impossible for the religious mind to understand. Destiny is greater than your history. It seems as if the great exchange of salvation is too good to be true. God gave us his best and took our mess, by putting it under the blood of Jesus. This is why the gospel is called the *good news.* In Christ all past, present, and future fires are all extinguished through repentance. Nothing can hold you back from your destiny.

Just because you've had a fall, doesn't mean that God's purpose for your life is over. You are the only one that can detour you from destiny. If your life seems to be a total mess, or a total wreck, this doesn't mean that your life is impossible for God to salvage. God specializes in trauma cases! God has a way of turning your mess into a masterpiece, trails into triumphs and your test into a testimony.

We all deserve the penalty of eternal damnation. *"But God demonstrates His own love toward us, in that while we were still sinners, Christ died for us."* Romans 5:8 NKJV. I am so glad that our future in Christ is not based on past performance. If so, none of us would qualify. *"Here in is love, not that we loved God, but that He loved us, and sent his Son to be the propitiation, for our sins."* I John 4:10.

We all have missed the mark one time are another. God doesn't deal with us according to our sins We embrace God's goodness. *"For all have sinned, and come short of the glory of God."Romans 3:23.* His favor is an act of His goodness that He gives to us in spite of us. *"The Lord is merciful and gracious; slow to anger, and*

85

abounding in mercy. He will not always strive with us. Nor will He keep His anger forever. " Psalms 103:89.

God is not up in heaven sitting on His throne waiting to strike you with a bolt of lightning every time you mess up or when you do something wrong. Remember we don't serve an angry God. *"As a father pities, his children, so the Lord pities those who fear Him. For He knows our frame: He remembers that we are dust."* Psalms 103:13-14 NKJV.

When we mess up, God doesn't want us running away from Him, but rather running to him. *"Let us therefore come boldly unto the throne of grace, that we may obtain mercy, and find grace to help in the time of need."* Hebrews 4:16. The shed blood of Jesus cleanses you of the past and gives you a position in God that is present. This position in God is equal to that of Jesus. Through the blood of Jesus, you can live without the sense of condemnation, guilt, fear, shame, or inferiority. Knowing this salvation process, you can maintain a conscience of righteousness. You will be able to live and operate even as Jesus lived and operated. It will not be hard for you to believe.

I get so excited every time I read the high priestly prayer that Jesus prayed. *"That they all may be one as You, Father, are in me, and I in You: that they also may be one, as You, that the world may believe that You sent me. "And the glory which You gave me I have given them, that they may be one just as We are one. I in them, and You in Me: that they may be made perfect in one, and that the world may know that You have sent Me, and loved them as You have loved me."* John 17:22-23 NKJV. God's Spirit comes and takes up residence in our recreated spirit. *"Do you not know that you are the temple of God and that the Spirit of God dwells in you?* I Corinthians 3:16 NKJV. The bible says, *For a just man falleth seven times, and riseth up again:* Proverbs 24:16.

Maurice Williams

Chapter 6
Seeing Through the Victory of Faith

This chapter was inspired by a young lady who is a member of our church. When I arrived home from the hospital, Margaret Parris gave me a cap with this saying on it, Man of Faith!. This cap reminded me of who I am. *"Now faith is the substance of things hope for the evidence of things not seen."*Hebrews 11:1. Faith gives us access into His grace, which is the channel that flows from all that God has for us. *"Without faith it is impossible to please Him; for he that cometh after God must believe that He is, and that He is a rewarder, of them that diligently seek Him."* Hebrews 11:6.

Grace is God's unmerited, favor. It is His mercy and goodness towards us. We can't do anything to achieve it neither can we do anything to accomplish it. We don't deserve it, he gives it to us as a favor. *"For by grace are ye saved through faith: and that not of yourselves: it is the gift of God; not of works, lest any man should boast."* Ephesians 2:8-9.

"For I say through the grace given unto me, to every man that is among you, not to think of himself more highly than he ought to think; but to think soberly, according as God has dealt to every man the measure of faith." Romans 12:3 .

89

If you've been born again, God has given you his faith in seed form. In order to get the results you desire, this faith must be cultivated. *"We are bound to thank God always for you, brethren, as it is meet because that your faith growth exceedingly, and the charity of every one of you all toward each other aboundeth."* 2 Thessalonians 1:3. It doesn't matter how far you've been set back; the revelation of the word of faith will be the light that will cause you to see your way out. With faith you can start over, rebuild, because it inspires your expectation. As long as there is breath in your body, there is hope.

As you see through the eyes of faith, the impossible becomes possible. *"Is there anything too hard for the Lord?" Ah, Lord God! Behold thou hast made the heaven and the earth by thy great power and stretched out arm, and there is nothing too hard for thee:* Jeremiah 32:17. As your faith grows, you are able to move any mountain on every level. If we live by faith we will not have to live from miracle to miracle, but rather from principle to principle. Faith will be a way of life. Many live their lives needing a miracle. Every month or every week or every day; they need a miracle. People of faith don't chase miracles. Miracles follow people of faith. Yes, miracles still happens!

Before Jesus went to the cross, he told those needing a miracle; *"be it unto you according to your faith."* On other occasions He would say," *your faith has made you whole."*

After his resurrection, we now live by the faith of the Son of God. Apostle Paul wrote to the Galatians and said; *I am crucified with Christ; Nevertheless I live; yet not I but Christ liveth in me. And the life that I now live in the flesh, I live by the faith of the Son of God. Who loved me, and gave himself for me.*"Galatians 2:20. So we do not live by any faith of our own, neither do we live by any righteousness of our own.

Only by the shed blood of Jesus are we made righteous. *"For He hath made (Jesus) him to be sin for us who knew know sin; that we might be made the righteousness of God in, him.*"II Corinthians 5:21. Apostle Paul addresses the church at Corinth on righteousness and the church at Galatians on The Son of God's faith. We are made the righteousness of God in Christ. Righteousness means that we are in right standing with God. We are justified by faith. Just as if we have never sinned. We have God's DNA. When you have righteousness and faith, you are unstoppable.

When faith takes root in your heart in abundance, you will release it out of your mouth. *"For of the abundance of the heart his mouth speaketh."* Luke: 6:45. God did not create the heart to function inoperative of the mouth. In faith, the heart and the mouth functions together. Faith has a voice. *"But the righteousness which is of faith speaketh on this wise."* Romans 10:6. Genuine faith will always speak. Faith has its own language. As faith grows in your heart, its belief will come out of your mouth. You will not be able to contain it, because true faith grows. This is how God designed the word of faith system to function.

This spirit (attitude) of faith is a mouth and heart connection that cannot be separated. You cannot have one without the other. This is one way of knowing that you are operating in the God kind of faith. *"We having the same spirit of faith according as it is written, I believed and therefore have I spoken we also believe and therefore speak."* II Corinthians 4: 13.

If it is in your heart in abundance, rest assure that it is going to come out of your mouth. You can say things with your tongue and not have the faith for it in your heart, but there is no way you can have faith in your heart in abundance, and it not come out of your mouth. Once faith takes root in your heart, *your tongue will be the pen of a ready writer* Psalms 45:1. Your faith can create your future with your tongue. There is a strong relationship between the mouth and the heart that will bring every desire into manifestation.

As you see in Romans 10:9-10. There is a relationship between the mouth and the heart. *"That if thou shalt confess with thy mouth the Lord Jesus and shalt believe in thy heart that God hath raised him from the dead, thou shalt be saved. For with the heart man believeth, unto righteousness: and with the mouth, confession is made unto salvation."* Here we see the connection of the heart and mouth again.

One day the apostles asked Jesus *"Lord increase our faith." And Jesus replied "If you have faith as a grain of mustard seed, ye might say unto this sycamine, tree, be thou plucked up by the root, and be thou planted into the sea: And it should obey you."* Luke 17:6. Notice what Jesus said to his disciples, if you had faith you would say or speak to the sycamine tree. Yes, He was speaking about a literal tree. This tree represents negative issues that are in your life. Because of the faith deposited in your heart you will speak to those issues.

I would like to give you another scripture that connects the mouth and the heart. It is a very familiar passage *"And Jesus saith unto them, have faith in God. For whosoever shall say unto this mountain be thou removed and be thou cast into the sea: And shalt not doubt in his heart, but shall believe that those things which he saith shall come to pass, he shall have whatsoever he saith. Therefore I say unto you, what things so ever ye desire when you pray believe that ye receive them and ye shall have them"* Mark 11: 22-24. In Mark chapter 11, verse 23, Jesus uses the word say three times. He uses the word heart one time. I believe that The Holy Spirit influenced the translators to compile the words say and heart by putting them in the same verse. I believe that God wanted us to know that there is a connection between the mouth and the heart, in order to operate in this God kind of faith. Faith connects the unseen realm with the seen realm.

Faith has no limits! It can go beyond natural boundaries. With faith, there is always an open door. Faith can bypass the natural process of things. There is always a yes when it comes to faith. *"All the promises of God are yes and in Him amen unto the glory of God by us"* II Corinthians 1:20   Again, faith is the door which opens and accesses the fullness of God or the grace of God. When you discover this door, you will also find out that *"Every good gift and every perfect gift is from above; and cometh down from the Father of lights, with whom is no variableness, neither shadow of turning."* James 1:17. Faith accesses this door to everything good and perfect that has been prepared for you and I before the foundation of the world.

Don't allow not having enough money, or not having any money stop you from taking a step of faith. It doesn't cost you anything to believe. "You don't need the money, until you need the money." *Come, every one that thirsteth, come ye to the waters, and he that no money; come, buy and eat: yea come, buy wine and milk without money and without price."* Isaiah 55:1. Again" you don't need the money until you need the money." In the natural realm, you need money in order to make a transaction, not so in the kingdom. In the kingdom, you don't need any money, because the word of faith is the currency of the kingdom in order to make any transaction. The money will manifest at the appointed time.

Faith has vision. It can visualize farther than the natural eyes can see. If you have faith for it, vision will be the vehicle that will bring you to it. Faith will bring what you are believing God for, out of the spirit realm into the natural realm. Faith inspires expectation! It comes by hearing the word of God. The more you hear (understand) and obey, the more your faith will grow. God created the world with words and you are creating your world with words. You determine your season for restoration and acceleration as you increase your sensitivity of hearing from the Holy Spirit. *"Then He said to them, take heed what you hear. With the same measure you use, it will be measured to you; and to you who hear; more will be given."* Mark 4:24 NKJV

Faith operates in the eternal now. This means that faith operates today, not tomorrow, not next week or next year, **but right now**! Remember this, Faith is Always Now! As you operate in faith, you will always see things as now. *"While we look not at the things that are seen, but at the things that are not seen: for the things which are seen are temporal: but the things which are not seen are eternal."* 2 Corinthians 4:18. As you operate in the God kind of faith, people will say things like: *'You are cocky, arrogant, boastful, or you think you're all that'.* They don't understand that faith gives you a Holy boldness. *"Where is boasting then? It is excluded. By* *what law? Of works? No; but by the law of faith"* Romans 3:27. The people of faith are not cocky, arrogant, or boastful. They're not afraid to speak the word of God. By speaking the word of God, sets this law in motion. Faith is a law; it is the word of truth over fact or reality.

Romans 12 verse 3 says; *"God hath dealt to every man the measure of faith."* God gives a measure to everyone to become a believer.

Those who are not led of the Holy Spirit operate from their senses and are led of the flesh. *"For they that are after the flesh do mind the things of the flesh: but they that are after the Spirit the things of the Spirit."* Romans: 8:5. Faith only functions in the spirit realm. You can't see, taste, smell, touch, or hear it, because it doesn't function in the realm of the senses. God communicates to you through your spirit. Whatever he says to you will never make sense, it only makes faith. You can only receive it by faith.

Having a consciousness of sin will cancel out the prayer of faith. This will strip you of your faith every time. You must maintain a conscience of righteousness, so that your faith can work. The nature of God is righteousness!
"For all unrighteousness is sin." 1 John 5:17. Unrighteousness produces lies, unbelief, religion, hate, fear, shame, condemnation, unforgiveness, worry,

inferiority, offense, and anything that is not the nature of God.

God has given us faith to overcome every situation in life. Faith can conquer everything. *"For whatever is born of God overcomes the world. And this is the victory that has overcome the world - our faith."* I John 5:4 Faith is not limited by what is on paper. Faith is not dependent on what you have in the bank. God has given you the victory of faith for every area of your life. Worship is also a high form of faith. Worship will cause your faith to thrive.

You are designed to go in the direction where you are able to see. This is where revelation comes in. Revelation causes you to see and believe the impossible; it makes faith easy to access the fullness of God. Faith will see the end of a thing, from its beginning and declare the outcome. This is why I am saying, you must see it before you *can see it*. If you see it through the victory of faith, it won't be long before you see its manifestation. The very word of faith you are standing on will become tangible.

Faith is an explosive force, dynamic in its working. It will rearrange any circumstance, crisis, trial, or impossibility. The Word of God is the substance of things hoped for and the evidence of things not governed by the senses. Faith is a lifestyle and the just shall live by faith.

You cannot feel faith. Faith is not a feeling because faith is a force that comes out of your spirit. In order for faith to work, you must leave the realm of the senses. Again, you can't hear, smell, touch, see or taste it. Faith is spirit bag, which holds words. *"It is the spirit that quickeneth: the flesh profiteth nothing; the words I speak unto you, they are spirit, and they are life."* John 6:63.

To overcome any impossibility that you are confronted with you need to go to the Word of God and find the promise for that impossibility. You need to remember that promise, meditate on that promise, chew on that promise, and speak that promise daily. As you do this, you are converting the promises into faith. You will be able to see the scriptures even with your eyes closed. This is how your victory of faith is manifested. You can never rise above the level of your faith confession.

The promise is the answer and the truth about that impossibility. It is far, far above any reality or fact that you may be currently experiencing. Faith can override anything, it can conquer anything, and overcome anything. *"And this is the confidence that we have in him, if we ask anything according to his will, he heareth us: and if we know that he hear us, whatsoever we ask, we know that we have the petitions we desired of him."* 1 John 5:14-16

Again, faith is a law. A law is a principle based on a predictable thing of an act. For example, if you do this;

you'll receive that. And if you do that you'll receive the rewards from it either good or bad.

Faith is predictable, it always declares the end of a thing from its beginning. Faith declares the outcome of the battle before it begins. *"The battle is not yours, but God's." Now thanks be unto God which always causes us to triumph in Christ".* II Corinthians 2:14. With the faith principle, you can always predict what's going to happen and what the outcome is going to be.

Maurice Williams

Chapter 7
Turning the Page to the Vision and Restoration

"We walk by faith and not by sight" II Corinthians 5:7

The enemy of vision is sight, sight is seen with your eyes, and vision is seen with your heart.

"I will stand upon my watch and set me upon the tower, and will watch to see what he will say unto me, and I shall answer when I am reproved. *And the Lord answered me, and said, write the vision, and make it plane upon tables, that he may run that readeth it; for the vision is yet for an appointed time, but at the end it shall speak, and not lie: Though it tarry, wait for it, because it shall surely come, it will not tarry."* Habakkuk 2:1-3.

After having the AVM of the brain, there was a strong possibility of me becoming paralyzed on one side of my body. In addition, I could have developed slurred speech, spinal cord damage, a twisted mouth, brain damage, and double vision. By the grace of God, I didn't experience any of those things. The doctors said this was unusual. This was a miracle in itself. The hospital staff said I should knock on wood. I asked my children what does" knock on wood" mean? My son who we call big Mesh said; "daddy when they say knock on wood, that means God saved you this time but next time if it happens, He may not save you. I began to laugh because that was so funny to me, and I said that is not even biblical. I would look at my condition, and tell myself; I will get back and go far beyond where I was. Faith with vision has allowed me to see the restoration. Yes, I saw myself doing what I use to do, and I see myself doing bigger and better things. The future is inside of my heart. It is God's eternal past. I've got to walk out what God has already finished.

I'm happy to announce that I am only taking two of the fourteen medications that the doctor has prescribed for me daily. Had I continued on the path with these medications, it would have costs me over $1000 month. I know different people have different opinions about prescription drugs. Some prescription drugs, such as painkillers, can be addictive. There are many who believe that if you are taking any prescription medication, you're not trusting God. I believe that you must be led by the Holy Spirit. I thank God by faith I no longer have to continue all the medications that were prescribed to me. This doesn't mean that you should get off your medication. You must be led by the Holy Spirit and let Him tell *you* what to do. By faith and soon, I will no longer have to take the remaining two prescription drugs. The Spirit of God is leading me, and at the appointed time, my doctor shall confirm this!

Pastor Rod and Joni Parsley were led by the Holy Spirit when they released their faith for their son's healing. Several years ago, their son Austin was diagnosed with a neurological, disorder called Asperger Syndrome. I heard Mrs. Joni Parsley say that God spoke to her and said "mix your heavenly resources with your earthly resources for your son's healing." Doctors and medicine was the earthly resource. This is why you should be led by the Holy Spirit, because God may tell you to do something different. Jesus didn't heal everyone the same. He didn't heal every blind person the same. What is God saying to you?

When I began writing this book, I was so empty. I felt as if someone had knocked the wind out of me. Have you ever felt you have been abandoned? I had to stay focused, to keep from being angry with God, and people. People criticized me for not having the faith to keep this from happening to me. After having the AVM of the brain, it seemed as if all visions and dreams that God had given me died. I had no fight in me. I didn't have any spiritual energy. I felt spiritually drained. I didn't sense the presence of God anymore. There were days I couldn't even put my words together to pray. My wife would have to pray for me. The most difficult times were when I would wake up and didn't even know what day it was, saying things that were irrelevant and talking out of my head.I would drive trying to make it to a certain destination only to end up on the other side of town because my brain was still shrinking. Bishop Steve Houpe would tell me, "You really need to be still. You don't want to experience a relapse." I thank God that

Lady Holly and Church Triumphant was patient with me, when I had these moments.

So, one day by faith I sat down and began to write this book. Three months past, I didn't sense His presence. Six months passed, I had no passion to write. But, I kept writing by faith. Faith is not a feeling. One day, I sensed the presence of God for this book. I had a passion to write. If I was going to see restoration, I had to look past my current condition, and turn the page to the vision and restoration.

His presence began to revive me, and energize me; vision and dreams came alive again. At this stage in my life, I'm only reaching for the things which are before me. I am only interested in walking the path to restoration, purpose, and destiny.

Restoration is an act of God's grace and favor toward us. We don't deserve it. Restoration is defined as something that needs to be restructured, reconstituted, or brought back into new alignment. It goes beyond that which was lost.

If you have no vision, you don't know where you're going. If you don't know where you are going any road will take you there. Vision gives you direction; it will also cause you to impose restrictions on yourself. This is known as discipline.

There were five things in my life, I had to resist after coming home from the hospital. Those five things worked overtime on me to try to get me in unbelief. Being in the state of unbelief, would have pushed me out of the will of God. These five things were; fear, self-pity, offense, grief and thoughts of dying. There was this fear of having another (AVM) stroke. There were days my wife had to leave the house and go shopping, attend to her mother, or go take care of some business. I would have to remain home. I really felt safe when Lady Holly was home with me, just in case I would have another AVM. I would keep the front door unlocked in case the paramedics were called to the house. I'm just keeping it real! If I went to the basement, or a certain place in my home, I would keep my cell phone with me; in the event I was faced with another AVM. I was looking more at the problem. This caused me to become fearful. One day I said; "enough is enough." I stood up to the bully of fear. I said to that intimidator, "You will not run my life another day." I began to cast down and resist the thoughts of fear.

By human nature, the process and problems were very challenging for me. I had to release faith for the grace in that situation. This is how I began to run the fear out of my life. I would declare; *"God has not given us the Spirit of fear; but of power, love and of a sound mind."*
II Timothy 1:7.

In February of 2013, Dr. Michael Abraham performed an angiogram. The test was completed and the screening revealed that I should never have this problem again. "Praise God."

The second thing I had to resist was self-pity. I can tell you that it is easier to just throw in the towel and give yourself a pity party, rather than believe God for a miracle. It was hard for me to believe that I was confronted with self-pity. Feeling helpless and hopeless brought about self-pity. I had many opportunities to get into self-pity. I would remember the time when it seemed I was on top of the world. Having a thriving church, a great big beautiful home, preaching many different places, everything was going so great.

I did not want to go out in public and be seen on a walker. People would see me and just stare and feel sorry for me. I didn't realize feeling this way, I was in self-pity. One day after attending the home going service of my good friend Pastor Kevin Vernon, I believe his passing was premature. He died at an early age. Pastor Tony and Lady Ann Cobbins took my wife and I to one of my favorite restaurants. The dinner date made me feel special. It gave me the encouragement that I needed to go out in public again.

While at dinner, First Lady Ann Cobbins asked me, "When you were unconscious, did you see Jesus or a light?" I replied, "No, I didn't see Jesus or a light. But in my spirit I wanted to be with Him." God gave me an unexplainable peace that I had not experienced before.

Along with seeing the vision and the restoration, comes a hope. I had to get out of my feelings. When you have hope, you care less about what others think or say. You must make sure that you are delivered from you. *"And hope maketh not ashamed; because the love of God is shed abroad in our hearts by the Holy Ghost which is given to us."* "Romans 5:5. Vision and restoration is conceived by hope.

The third thing I had to resist was offense. I really had to guard my heart against this one. *"Then said He unto his disciples. It is impossible but that offenses will come; but woe unto him through whom they come!* Luke 17:1. Offense comes from the Greek word skandalon[2]. Skandalon means; the triggers in a trap on which bate is placed. The springs on the trap are activated when the prey touches it, causing it to close. The trap goes undetected and unnoticed because the hunter camouflages it. The trap is to bring injury, suffering, and pain to the prey.

I've preached to others about not becoming offended, and in this case; I was being confronted with offense. *"A brother offended is harder to be won than a strong city: and their contentions are like the bars of a castle."* Proverbs 18:19. I knew one thing, if I loved God there could be no room for offense. I would resist thoughts of blaming God, and developing a bad attitude against him for what happened to me. I had to constantly cast down these negatives imaginations and say out loud *'God has not done anything wrong. God loves me and God is good to me.'* One of the most challenging things for me was watching my wife and children having to cope with this restoration process. As I was going through the process of the pain and suffering, my family was feeling the pressure of it also.

Vision is purpose when you can see it. You give your children vision, when you find your purpose. Vision is never personal, it is always generational. *"And it shall come to pass in the last days, saith God, I will pour out my Spirit upon all flesh: and your son's and your daughters shall prophesy, and your young, men shall see visions, and your old men shall dream dreams: And on my servants and on my handmaidens I will pour out in those days of my Spirit; and they shall prophesy:"* Acts 2: 17-18.

For the old men a dream is a vision that they may not see in their lifetime, yet it is passed down to generations so that they will help bring the dream to pass.

My children did not want to see me in pain. They wondered where the Almighty God was in all of this! God could have prevented all of this from happening! We dealt with the situation as best we could. Many times, we really couldn't say much about everything we were dealing with as a family. We would leave home and go to church, shopping, or other places with a smile on our faces, but on the inside, we were all hurting.

I would over hear my children say things like, "I don't want to have anything to do with ministry anymore." This is not the attitude of my children only. The majority of Pastors kids feel this way. Preacher kids see and hear all the misunderstandings, the offenses, the pain and hurt of things their parents go through in ministry. They would say, "just look at what happened to Daddy."

Seeing what I was going through was like a dart going through their hearts, therefore they didn't want anything to do with ministry. I raised them to love and serve God. I didn't say that they had it altogether. They are like other children. Yes, they have made mistakes, but their hearts have always been in pursuit of God. All they have ever known is God. *"Lo, children are an inheritance of the Lord: and the fruit of the womb is his reward. As arrows are in the hand of a mighty man: So are children of thy youth."* Psalms 127:3-4.

I had to minister to their hearts by telling them to protect their hearts and not to become callas against God. I would constantly talk with them and say I'm alright, please don't develop a hard heart against God. Don't become offended at God. God has done nothing wrong. Watch and see for yourselves that God is bringing good out of this situation. I would pray that God would remove from them a heart of stone (offense) and replace it with a heart of flesh that will serve God no matter what!

The fourth thing I had to resist was grief. Grief is usually a season that you go through at the passing of a love one. Grief can also be associated with any type of loss. I had to resist grief for the loss of the church building and the loss of my health. Grief is a reality. But I had to resist its' right to control my life. The things and the relationships that I was attached and connected with were now gone. This season of grief would try to overwhelm me. Nevertheless, I had to stand up to this bully.

On May 27, 2014, my nephew (Kamal Bensahri) passed away. His passing was premature. It shocked the whole family. He was like a son to me. I have two sons, when you would see them, you saw Kamal. His passing was so sudden. The grief tried to overwhelm us. Grief will always bring on stress, depression, sadness, and heaviness. We had to immediately resist grief. Yes, we experienced sorrow. But we did not sorrow as those who have no hope. Our hope is in Christ. Kamal was from a beautiful, single-parent home. I miss him to this very day. There will always be a special place in my heart for Kamal. He will be truly missed. I remember one day when we were leaving church, Kamal said, "uncle Maurice, you seem like a father to me." His words really touched my heart.

The fifth thing I had to resist were thoughts of dying. I kept the vision before me so I could experience my full restoration. The vision will live far beyond my generation. It will be active until Jesus comes.

Regardless of all that has happened, I was still holding on to what God had promised me. I've turned the page on the sickness, all the losses, fear, self-pity, offense, relationships, grief and thoughts of dying. I'm turning the page to the next chapter of my life. God always restores better than it was before. I'm receiving double for all the trouble. Before I was released from the hospital, my doctor asked me if my church was one of those churches that has a lot of excitement. "I said yes it sure does." The doctor advised me if I attended church to stay for only one hour, after that I must leave. "Do not speak, greet, or interact with the people, because my brain is still shrinking." I attended church but I did not preach until I got the green light from my doctor. It would be six months before I would step back into the pulpit. I am back preaching, but I'm taking it easy. According to the doctor, I am still not operating at 100%. I would say my level of operating is somewhere around 75%.

Different Pastors would come by on Sunday morning and on Wednesday night for our midweek services to deposit a word in the ministry. Great men and women would take time out of their busy schedules and minister to Church Triumphant World Overcomers

International. We are grateful for these Pastors and Ministers that preached in my absence for the six-month period. I would like to say special thanks to:

- *Lady Holly Williams of Church Triumphant World Overcomers International, Kansas City, MO*
- *Pastor T. J. Huskey of Church Triumphant World Overcomers International, Kansas City, MO*
- *Pastor Tony Cobbins of Canaan Worship Center, Kansas City, MO*
- *Associate Pastor Ruben Johnson of Apostolic Church Of Jesus Christ of Kansas City, MO*

- *Pastor Phillip Steele of Faith Builders International, DeSoto, KS*
- *Minister Maurice Martin Harvest Church of Kansas City, MO*
- *Pastor Erick Vassol, Living Word Grandview MO*
- *Dr.Elverta Vassol Assitan Pastor, Living Word Grandview MO*
- *Pastor Dassie Summers, Memorial Outreach, Kansas City, MO*
- *Pastor Randolph Cobbins, Big Vision Church, North Kansas City, MO*
- *Assistant Pastor Lady Michelle Woods, Urban Empowerment Ministry, Columbia Mo*
- *Pastor David Walker of Faith Christian Center, Leavenworth KS*
- *Pastor Jessie Thomas, In God Hands Ministry, Kansas City, MO*

- *Pastor Eric Cobbins, The Worship Center of Kansas City, Lenexa KS*
- *Pastor Greg Hall, New Season , Kansas City MO*
- *Minister LaVonda Graham, Church Triumphant World Overcomers International , Kansas City MO*

I am most grateful for their service to our ministry. During those six months, I was unable to preach, yet the vision was still alive in me. Vision is having foresight into the future, conceiving what God has called you to do to fulfill His purpose; *"Where there is no vision, the people perish: but he that keepth the law, happy is he."* Proverbs 29:18. Vision is the transportation that will give you a lift to your destiny.

Where there is vision, there will be provision and discipline. Vision will embrace laws and principles that will produce joy, happiness, and satisfaction. Vision will also bring about order; you will set boundaries and goals for your life, ministry, family, and business.

Faith is the present and vision is the future. I kept the vision before me; this helped me to see restoration. We are also appreciative to Bishop John L. Brown and the New Landmark Worship Center for allowing Church Triumphant to worship in their strip mall, a couple of Sundays when we had nowhere to worship.

Right now, I'm living in between the restoration and the vision. I would like to say I am in transition. I'm not where I would like to be; I thank God I'm not where I use to be. I am not complaining because I'm not where I would like to be. I am somewhere in the middle, being restored from all losses, and I am on my way to destiny. Our Church ministry is currently worshipping in a building that is 25,000 square feet. My wife and I have another home that we are living in only by the grace of God. Pastor Tony Cobbins and the Canaan Worship Center of Kansas City opened their Young Nation Building to us and God is restoring us there. The church ministry is growing again. The ministry is healthy and whole. The people are excited, and there is great joy in the house!

 While trying to get up from the fall and make a comeback, everything that was established in my life had crumbled. I am still here today only because of His grace, mercy and purpose. Many didn't make it, it's a miracle that I did. When Jacob received news that he didn't want to hear he said *"all these things are against me."* I felt that everything was working against me but in actuality, they were working for my good. At the time, it didn't seem like it, but it was in fact working for my good! I would also like to say a special thank you to all those who disowned me, discredited me, criticized me, and left me for dead. The word in the Christian community was, I had died. It has all given me the power and strength to turn the page to God's bigger plan for my life. *It is good for me that I have been afflicted; that I might learn thy statutes.* Psalm 119:71.

I held to the anchor of faith, so I wouldn't drift away. No matter what it looked like, and no matter what was going on, the promise is *"I will never leave you nor forsake you."* No matter how low I got, the word of God assured me that God still had a purpose for me. No matter how bad things are in your life, God still has a purpose, and a plan for your life. *"And we know that all things work together for the good of them, that love God, to them who are the called according to His purpose."* Romans 8:28. It doesn't work for everyone. Remember it only works out for the good of them who loves God. It may not feel good at that very moment, but God will bring good from it. He will make it good for you and set you on the road to destiny. God will not allow the devil to have the last word.

Worship is a part of my life. I would feed my spirit, spiritual food. This is what sustained me. *"The spirit of a man will sustain his infirmity; but a wounded spirit who can bear?"* Proverbs 18:14.

After the AVM, I was not able to lay prostrate before the Lord; however, I would sit in my favorite chair at home to pray and worship. We are all created to worship, and live out our son-ship here on earth. My relatives told me while I was heavily sedated in the intensive care unit, I was worshipping God; lifting my hands as I laid flat on my back in my hospital bed. Of course, I don't remember any of this. The only answer that I can give for this is the worshipper (Holy Ghost) was on the inside of me. When you are a worshipper, it is not predicated on how things are going in your life, if you are doing well or not. Worship is what we do. *"God is a spirit: and they that worship him must worship him, in spirit and truth."* John 4:24.

Faith, revelation, restoration, purpose, and destiny kept me motivated. I appreciate the encouragement, all the supportive words, and all the things that people had done to help me get back on the road to recovery, purpose, and destiny. Revelation made it easier for me to see my future. Once you get a revelation for your situation, it will make what you believing God for very easy. Along with faith and favor, all toil will be taken away. Jesus said, *"my yoke is easy and my burden is light."*

Before Jesus ascended on high, he transferred authority into the hands of the church. *"Verily, verily I say unto you, He that believeth on me, the works that I do shall he do also; and greater works than these shall he do; because I go unto my Father."* John 14:12. We are Christ representatives in the earth. We are His hands, feet, voice extended. *"For whom he did foreknow, he also did predestinate to be conformed to the image of his Son, that he might be the firstborn among many brethren. Moreover whom he did predestinate, them he also called: and whom he called, them he also justified: and whom he justified, them he also glorified."* Romans 8:29-30. Another scripture declares, *"For we are his workmanship, created in Christ Jesus unto good works, which God hath before ordained that we should walk in them."* Ephesians 2:10.

My destiny is much greater than the AVM. If the aneurysm did not kill me, that simply means that God has purposed me for His next diminutive season. This is why I can turn the page to the vision and restoration.

Now it's high time for you to turn the page on the rape, incarceration, racism, hatred, unforgiveness, broken relationships, foreclosure, alcoholism, addictions, divorce, abortion, sickness, and all the things that may have set you back. You are trying to explain why you are having a difficult time turning the page. You have heard that same old song before, "JUST GET OVER IT."

You might be criticized for not having turned the page. People think you should be over it by now. They don't know like you know. It eats at you constantly. You truly want to turn the page on it, but you don't know how. Instead of addressing this problem, you just suppress it. You are crying out for help because you really don't know how to turn the page on the past, so that you can go to the future of the next level. There are those who say, "just turn the page." This is easier said than done trust me I know.

Whatever happened in the past may or may not be the results of your actions. Weather it is or not, you still don't have to be a victim of your past. The spirit of condemnation will yoke you, to keep you bound to the past. It will make you feel unworthy and unacceptable for the grace of God. Remember the enemy is in your past, but God is in your future. Your future is much brighter than your past.

If you are going to turn the page on all bad things, you must first know that God is love. Not that God has love, but that HE is love. His love is unconditional. One of the attributes of love is forgiveness. When you embrace the love of God, you have automatically embraced forgiveness. Know that nothing from the past can hold you. The reason why you have not turned the page is because somewhere you are walking in condemnation, feeling sorry for yourself, and unforgiveness. One of the hardest things to do is to forgive <u>yourself</u>. You must forgive <u>yourself;</u> not forgiving yourself is a sin. Once you get a revelation on the love of God you will be able to turn the page on the past, and turn to an awesome future which is the next chapter of your life.

Hurt and pain does not discriminate. It comes in all shapes, sizes, and colors. It comes to the rich and to the poor alike. It doesn't have respecter of persons or status. As you get a revelation on the love of God, you will begin studying and meditating on the word of God and declaring everything that He has said about you. As you meditate on the promises of God, His life that is in you, will begin to emerge out of you. As you speak the word that Jesus has spoken for that situation, watch it change. *"Jesus said the words that; I speak unto you they are spirit and they are life."* John 6:63.

My advice to you is to fall in love with God. Remember God loves you where you are. God loves you, no matter what. Whatever the past may be, know that God is greater than your past. *"But where sin abounded, grace did much more abound."* Romans 5:20. Once you turn the page, get ready to be processed, so you can reach your destiny.

"For a just man falleth seven times, and riseth up again:" Proverbs 24:16.

Maurice Williams

Chapter 8
The Process

"Yea, though I walk through the valley of the shadow of death, I will fear no evil: for thou art with me: thy rod and thy staff they comfort me." Psalms 23: 4. Now we have come to the chapter that everyone would just like to skip over. No one likes to talk about or go through a process. Everyone loves to talk about and dream about potential, promise, purpose, destiny, and blessings. In this chapter, I talk about process. The process is what molds and shapes you so you will be able to handle your next level. It is like a metamorphosis that you must experience before you can go into your next dimension. Without process, there will be no transformation of becoming____! It comes to eliminate all dead weight and to empty you of yourself. Where God is taking you, old things cannot come. Don't view the valleys as the absence of God.

"And this word, yet once more, signifieth the removal of those things that are shaken, as of things that are made, that those things which cannot be shaken may remain." Hebrews 12:27. All that left me could not stay and all that stayed could not leave. You must stop looking at what you've lost and rejoice in what you have left. Process shakes everything and everyone around you; that when the dust settles whatever is left standing is what goes with you into the next dimension.

121

The valley that you are going through may be a process that God is using to get you to the promise and on to your destiny. I would like to say that valleys and mountains are only typologies of the processes and promises.

God always takes what Satan does and bring good from it, in order to direct those who love Him to their promise and destiny. It is like putting all the ingredients in a bowl for the batter to make a cake. When all the ingredients go into the bowl; the batter doesn't look anything what you envision for a finished cake. But you must begin to stir the batter, place it in the oven, and heat at a certain temperature for the cake to become what its' intended to be. Once the heat is applied, the batter is processed, and what you envisioned (the cake) begins to rise. All the ingredients have worked together for the good to bring about the cake. After Jesus was anointed, He too had to go through the process of resisting temptation in the wilderness, to get to the next dimension in the Spirit. *"And Jesus returned in the power of the Spirit into Galilee and there went out a fame of him through all the region round about."* Luke 4:14.

The promise is; we go from faith to faith, and glory to glory. Every believer will be processed before going to what God has next for him or her. God will not give you the promise without taking you through the process. God set the children of Israel free from bondage, after 430 years. He led them through the red sea and into the wilderness. He could have easily taken them directly to the land of promise. The reason why he didn't was that they had not been processed for the promise. Even though God had relocated them from Egypt to the wilderness, they still had the mindset of Egypt in them. God allowed them to go through a forty-year process, until all that mindset of Egypt was dead. When that old mindset was dead, then God was able to take them to the promise.

"Now after six days Jesus took Peter, James, and John his brother, led them up on a high mountain by themselves; and He was transfigured before them. His face shone like the sun, and His clothes became as white as the light. And behold Moses and Elijah appeared unto them talking with him. Then Peter answered and said to Jesus, "Lord it is good for us to be here: if you wish, let us, make here three tabernacles: one for you, one for Moses, and one for Elijah" Matthew 17: 1-4 NKJV.

It was on the mountain that Peter opened his eyes and saw glory manifested. You may think that glory is only manifested on the mountain. God is not just God on the mountains, but He is also God of the valleys. When you are in a valley and things are not going right. The enemy will try to distract you from looking toward the God of deliverance. Remember God has given you victory down in the valley. God can manifest a miracle in your situation.

"And there came a man of God and spake unto the King of Israel, and said, Thus saith the Lord, because the Syrians have said, the Lord is God of the hills, but he is not God of the valleys, therefore I will deliver all this great multitude into thine hand, and ye shall know that I am the Lord." I Kings 20:28.

The evening of August 16, 2012, I was transported from the Menorah Hospital of Overland Park, Kansas; to the University of Kansas Hospital. Menorah Hospital could not perform this specific brain surgery that I needed. While transporting me, I did not remember anything because I was heavily sedated, so I wouldn't feel any pain.

While I was in transit to the hospital, disc jockey, Reggie Brown of the KGGN Radio Station announced to the Kansas City Metropolitan area that I had been rushed to the hospital because of a brain aneurysm. People came to the hospital from all over the city. A young woman that monitors the family waiting room told me that they were contemplating if they should shut down the waiting room or not because of the large number of people. They could not do this because this would have been illegal.

After having brain surgery, I didn't remember much of anything, not even family. I was able to remember Lady Holly, Bishop and Mrs. Steve Houpe, and The Covenant Alliance Ministry Pastors, former Kansas City Chiefs star, Eddie Kennison, Pastor Eric Cobbins, Pastor Homer Cross. I also remember having a visit from Apostle and Mrs. Larry Akins, Pastor Chauncey Dixon, Bishop Eric Morrison and Bishop Ervin Sims.

"Yea though I walk through the valley of the shadow of death, I will fear no evil." The Holy Spirit Himself is walking me through this valley process. The valley experience is not death. It is only a shadow. It may be a reality, but it is not the truth. We must go through a valley in order to get to the mountain of destiny. *"While we look not at the things that are seen, but the things that are not seen: for the things which are seen are temporal; but the things which are not seen are eternal."* II Corinthians 4:18. The seen things are temporary and subject to change. The unseen things are truth and eternal. There are two things that are always constant; they are truth and change. In the natural realm, change is always constant. This is why you cannot put your trust in things you can see. In the eternal realm, truth is always constant; this is why you can put your eyes on what you cannot see.

You must adapt to change. If you don't learn how to adapt, change could destroy you. When you are confronted with process, just adapt to it; and began to change so you can reach your destination. One of the most challenging things to do is change!

Whether the manifestation is instant or processed; it is

still a miracle. There are instant miracles and there are processed miracles. God is glorified in both. We use to sing a song back in the day that said these words; *"Anyway you bless me Lord I'll be satisfied"* Whether it is instantaneous or processed, I'll be satisfied. When you release your faith for a miracle, God knows which one to manifest in your life. He will give you just what you need.

Before Jesus went to Calvary, he went to the Garden called Gethsemane, better known as the oil press or the place of the crushing. This is where olives were picked and processed. After being processed there was pure, fresh oil. Some of the disciples had witness His transfiguration on the mountain, now they are about to witness His agony in the garden (valley). In this garden called Gethsemane, is where Jesus died to himself for Calvary. *"He went away again the second time and prayed, saying, O my Father if this may not pass away from me, except I drink it, Thy will be done. And he came and found them asleep again: for their eyes were heavy. And he left them, and went away again, and prayed the third time, saying the same words. Then cometh he to his disciples, and saith unto them, sleep on, now, and take your rest: Behold the hour is at hand, and the Son of man, is betrayed into the hands of sinners"* *Matthew 26: 42-45.* In Mark chapter 14 verse 36 Jesus was praying and he said *"Abba Father all things are possible unto thee take away this cup from me nevertheless not what I will but what thou wilt."*

The men and women of God that have great anointings on their lives and ministries have had some great adversity and challenges. Greatness doesn't come without a price. I would like to say it like this; the deeper the foundation, the higher the skyscraper; the greater the opposition; the greater the miracle. The greater the persecution, the greater the blessing.

In order to get fresh oil from an olive, it has to go through the process of being beaten and then crushed. The men and women that have fresh oil on their ministries somewhere in their lives have been crushed by a process to produce the fresh oil of anointing. Only those that have been crushed are the ones who are able to minister out from the anointing. God brings us through so that we can bring others through. You cannot minister effectively without the anointing. If you have not gone through a process there is really not much you can say effectively, without power.

We know the anointing to be the burden removing yoke destroying power of God. *"And it shall come to pass, that in that day, that his, burden shall be taken away from off thy shoulder and his yoke from off thy, neck, and the yoke shall be destroyed because of the anointing.* Isaiah 10:27 The anointing is not cheap. It will cost you everything. With the anointing, you are never spiritually depleted or empty. *"King David said thou anointest my head with oil my cup runneth over."* Psalms 23:5. You must protect and guard the anointing by not allowing others in your cup. The cup is for you to live everyday life. The overflow is for those whom you minister to. If you are ministering to people on any level, make sure that there is an overflow of the anointing to get the job done, whatever the God-given assignment may be. He is giving you the grace and the anointing to get the job done. He gives you the grace for the space. God's anointing and grace upon your life has equipped you for the assignment.

Jesus did not perform one miracle, teach, or preach until he was anointed. *"Now when all the people were baptized it came to pass that Jesus also being baptized and praying the heaven was open and the Holy Ghost descended in a bodily shaped like a dove up on him and a voice from heaven which said Thou art my beloved Son in whom: in thee I am well pleased."* Luke 1:21-22. Know your calling; know the assignment that God has anointed you for. Remember the anointing will not work if what you are doing is not within the assignment. *"How God anointed Jesus of Nazareth with the Holy Ghost and with power, who went about doing good, and healing all that were oppressed of the devil: for God was with him."* Acts 10:38. Remember the anointing will remain on you, if what you're doing is within the assignment. So stay in your lane. Don't try to do what others are doing. Only do what God has assigned you to do.

It is vital for us to know the person of Jesus, the presence of Jesus, the principles of Jesus, and the purpose of Jesus. God shows us how important it is to be anointed and to walk in our divine purpose. *"The spirit of the lord is upon me, because he has anointed me to preach the gospel to the poor: he had sent me to heal the broken hearted, to preach deliverance to the captives, and recovering of sight of them that are blind to set at liberty them that are bruised, to preach acceptable year of the Lord."* Luke 4:18.

Purpose is what you were created to do. Know your purpose. Know why you were birthed into this world. There are over seven billion people on this planet and many don't know why they were created. Purpose will always bring about peace, happiness, satisfaction, and fulfillment. Purpose must be discovered. It can even be discovered through pain persecution, hurt, trials, tribulations and setbacks, etc. Through your discovery, you will also find that you may have other gifts that are lying dormant on the inside of you.

The anointing is not just for the Apostle, Prophet, Evangelists, Pastor, or Teacher. There is an anointing for all to complete their God-given assignment. You have an advantage over others because you have the anointing. The anointing gives you a supernatural ability to do things that ordinarily you wouldn't be able to do. God will take you through a process to develop you for destiny. It is not something that you will just walk or fall into. Once you are prepared, the door to destiny will open to you. In other words, you will be mature enough where you can handle it. *"A Just man falleth seven times and riseth up again."* Proverbs 24:16 Falling down is not failure, staying down is.

I went to a restaurant one day to eat and to reflect on my life, health and ministry. I began thinking about how I almost died with the brain aneurysm, how that my equilibrium was not functioning properly, my balance was very unstable, and I had to walk with the assistance of a walker. I remember over the years, great international speakers coming to minister at our church. Great men and women such as Bishop Steve Houpe, Dr. Donna Houpe, Dr. Bill Winston, Dr. Creflo Dollar, Dr. Michael Freeman, Dr. Dee Dee Freeman, Bishop George Bloomer, Cynthia Brazelton, Bishop Clarence Williams, Apostle Skip Horton, Bishop Tony Cobbins, Pastor Dexter Howard, Bishop Donald Battle, Apostle Larry B. Akins, Apostle Keith Wesley, Dr. Nasir Siddiki, Pastor Isaac Pitre, Evangelist Willie Clinkscale, Prophet Kevin Leal, Bishop Ervin Sims and others. I was thinking about all of the outreach programs, Logos Academy, and all the people who got saved under our ministry. How could we pick up where we left off? It was an overwhelming thought.

There was tremendous concern with the loss of our church building. I thought constantly about having to sit for two years on my sofa unable to engage in any formal activities. I had so much to think about; being unable to drive, the heavy intake of medicine prescribed by my doctor (fourteen different prescription medications daily). All of this was weighing heavily on my mind. I had over a half of a million dollars in medical bills and the loss of hearing in my right ear. Legal issues surfaced concerning our mortgage loan and the unethical practices of inappropriate signatures. We had to move out of our home by the order of the court. The Judge issued us a settlement. The settlement offer was ok, but I would have rather remained in our home. On top of all this, people scattering from the ministry. My situation looked very, very hopeless. "I asked myself, how much more can one person take?"

During this time, the church was going from one hotel ballroom to another. We did this every Sunday morning and Wednesday night to hold the remnant together. Several members hung in there with my wife and I. This is why I say that the members of Church Triumphant World Overcomers International are some of the greatest members in the world. I would encourage those that remained, to hang in there. I also encouraged them not to allow the enemy to sever their connection from their Pastor or wife and Church Triumphant. The members could come out to church; however, I was still unable to preach.

My situation kind of reminds me of Ezekiel's vision, the valley of dry bones. *"And he said to me, Son of man can these bones live? So I answered, "O Lord God, thou knowest."* Ezekiel 37:3. In the vision, the prophet saw the bones of all those that died. The problem looked so bad that the prophet said, Lord, you know the answer to this one. If you are not careful, you will accept things just as they are, and say *"maybe it's just supposed to be this way"*. I am told when I was in a state of unconsciousness, many people, ministers, and relatives, saw my situation and concluded to my wife that this was the end. They wanted her to except death as the will of God. They assumed that the condition I was in was my final end. They judged me based on what they had seen and heard.

My wife and others believed God to raise me up and to restore me. *"I shall not die, but live, and declare the works of the Lord."* Psalm 118:17. In addition, I knew it wasn't my time to die I believe that the people of God will know the season when it is time to go and be with God. According to the scriptures, a saint will know when it is their season to go and be with the Lord.

There was a time that Apostle Paul was stoned and left for dead, he faced death, on different occasions, but he could not die because his assignment was not completed. In his last writing to his son Timothy, he knew that it was his time to go to be with Jesus. *"For I am now ready to be offered, and the time of my departure is at hand. I have fought a good fight, I have finished my course, I have kept the faith:* II Timothy 4: 6-7. *"Now the sons of the prophets who were at Jericho came to Elisha and said to him do you know that the Lord will take away your master from over you today so he answered yes I know keep silent!"* II Kings 2:5 NKJV.

This vision of the dry bones represented the nation of Israel. God was showing the prophet what was going to happen to the Jewish people. It was the devil's way of trying to exterminate the Jewish race. The bones of them were found in the consecration camps, gas chambers, and the graves. God had a plan to bring them out of their graves, and His plan, will always come to pass. God made a promise to Abraham concerning his seed, and in 1948 Israel was born again, to be a nation.

Just like Israel was restored to nation status. I knew I would be restored. I'm just walking out the everyday process. The moment I declared restoration out of my mouth, things begin to get in alignment. The orchestrating of restorations began to line up and come together.

I must say Lady Holly is the love of my life. She has been my inspiration. If it were not for her, I would be dead. *She's my ride or die lady!* I'm speaking of before and after the hospital stay. When I returned home from the hospital, there were things I had to continue doing just to stay alive. I know now that all of this was part of the process, "going through the valley of the shadow of death." One day God gave me a revelation and it was as if a light came on, that this comeback is not for me to try to make happen. It would take a miracle, an act of God's grace. Yes, it would have to be *"Not by might nor by power but by my spirit saith the Lord of hosts."* Zechariah 4:6. It is because there is a grace on my life for the restoration. While I was in the hospital, the Holy Spirit birthed in the heart of Apostle Larry B. Akins to have a special two-day Saturday and Sunday benefit service for our church.. The benefit services brought the Christian community together in the heart of Kansas City. The services crossed denominational lines, racial barriers, and different cultures for the glory of God. The Christian community came out to lift up the name of Jesus!

I would like to say a special thank you to all of the Apostles, Prophets, Bishops, Elders, Pastors, Ministers, and laymen for attending the services and making them a huge success. These benefit services put our ministry back on the road to recovery and purpose. Apostle Akins sent two of his armor bearers to my hospital room to hook up a special Internet connection so I could watch the Sunday evening service live via satellite in HD color.

I believe that God will send people in your life with a purpose for a season, which may not necessarily be connected to your destiny. If they are not connected with your destiny; they are only with you for a season. *"To everything, there is a season, and a time to every purpose under the heaven."* Ecclesiastes 3:1. When their season with you is over, the purpose for coming into your life is over. This is not to say that they are bad people, because they have exited your life. It is just that their purpose and season for coming into your life is over.

I also believe that there are those who are connected to your vision and destiny, however sometimes the devil brings offense to sever that connection to keep them from reaching their destiny. When this happens, God will raise up others and assign them to your vision, so you can keep going forward and not miss a beat.

"From that time many of his disciples went back and walked no more with him. Then said Jesus to the twelve, will ye also go away? Simon Peter answered him, Lord to whom shall we go? Thou hast the words of eternal life. And we believe and are sure that thou art the Christ, the Son of the living God." John 6:66-69. Peter and the disciples were connected to Jesus for destiny the reason why they couldn't walk away.

I could see the vision and the restoration coming to pass, I'm experiencing restoration however, I'm in transition. I'm not where I would like to be, but I'm not where I use to be. I thank God I'm somewhere in the middle, being restored from all losses, and I'm on my way to destiny. I would like to know, can you still praise God in the valley? Don't look at this valley that you're currently in as a negative thing. God will use the valley on your behalf and bring good from it. He is developing, molding, and shaping you while in the valley. Valleys will cause you to cry out to God. God will bring you through every one of them. The valley can be a lonely place. You really don't know what you're made of until you are in the valley. I know there is a teaching that says if you exercise faith in God, you will not have valleys or you will not have to deal with any sufferings. I believe that this is far from the truth. However, I do believe that when a child of God suffers; it's for the sake of Christ. There is a scripture that says, *"For I reckon that the sufferings of this present time are not worthy to be compared with the glory which shall be revealed in us."* Romans 8:18.

"But beloved think it not strange concerning the fiery trial which is to try you, as though some strange thing happened unto you: But rejoice and as much as you are partakers of Christ's sufferings that when his glory shall be revealed ye may be glad also with exceeding joy. If ye be reproach for the name of Christ happy are ye; for the spirit of glory and of God rested upon you: on their part he is evil spoken of, but on your part he is glorified. But let none of you suffer as a murderer, or as a thief, or an evildoer, or as a busybody, in other men's matters. Yet if any man suffer as a Christian let him not be a shame but let him glorify God on this behalf." I Peter 4: 12-16.

Anyone can praise God when things are going well. However, can you praise God when things are bad? If you praise God in the valley, you will not be there very long. Praise will bring you through the valley. When you praise God, He will come personally and sit on your situation. If God sits on your situation, get ready, because the change that you are hoping for is going to take place. The valley is an uncomfortable place, but while going through God will give you grace and peace during your valley process.

The process keeps you humble. You may not understand why you're going through the valley, and why you are being processed. Let me tell you, the process is only preparing you for God's original purpose and intent for your life that He has already spoken over you. His word will prevail; it will not fall to the ground, for it shall come to pass. If you focus on the promise, the process will pass.

Looking back over your life and all the bad things you have gone through, there is a reason why God allowed you to go that route. All that you went through then was only preparing, positioning and processing you for now. Yes, what you have gone through, may have been horrible but, you made it. Now it is time to live. God allowed it to happen, weather you know it or not, that thing has processed you, for an appointed time. So just, keep your eyes on the promise. If you are going to see the manifestation of the promise, you must guard against doubt and fear.

If you focus on the problem, there will be no

manifestation of the promise. Restoration is my present and future. The time for it, is now, I'm in the place for God's miracle restoration. I declare that I will have, I will see, and I will do more of the works of Jesus in my latter days than I did in my 30s and 40's. I had some amazing times in ministry in my 30s and 40s. "My latter shall be greater than my past."

I anticipate that the restoration will be "exceeding abundantly above all that I can ask or think, according to the power that worketh in me." God is giving me back things that I have lost. He is restoring to me old things, by replacing them with new things.

I'm not focused on the process or the problems. I'm focused on the promise. As I walk through the valley of the shadow of death, my heart will not fear. As I wait for the manifestation, I will not faint, loose courage, or quit. I am walking through this valley to get to the next dimension. In every process, God is stretching your soul's capacity to think for another level, to believe for another level. When you are walking by faith, you will never become satisfied where you are. Remember there is always more in God. God is applying the heat in the process and ironing out all the kinks and wrinkles so you can receive the next level. I know it does not feel good, nor does it seem good at the moment. It's not supposed to feel good neither will it ever seem good, but it's working for your good. My suggestion to you is to stay in faith and praise God in the process.

The process is not the devil, so don't rebuke the process. It is the very thing that God is using to develop you for greatness. Just because you have entered into a struggle or opposition don't think that it's the devil. You must go through in order to get to the promise of destiny. Destiny requires development and discipline so that God will be glorified.

On this particular day while in the hospital for some reason I was very agitated and complaining, to my nurse about not wanting to attend rehab class. The nurse came to me and said that the doctor has put in your schedule for you to attend rehab functions for the next three weeks. She said, "You must attend and participate." I told her, " I wasn't going nor did I want to be bothered today." I had developed an attitude because of the AVM.

My wife said to me, "Honey, you have to go to rehab! Don't you want to get better? You must go because of the insurance. You've got to go." So, I made up my mind and I agreed to attend the rehab class. When I got there I saw the physical therapist teaching this guy how to get in and out of the bed. The amazing thing about this guy is he had no arms and no legs. I saw this and I said, "Lord, forgive me for complaining." I said to myself, this guy is worse off than I am. "There's nothing so bad that it can't be worse."

Maurice Williams

Chapter 9
The Next Dimension

*"Behold the former things are come to pass, and new things do I declare: before they spring forth I tell you of them. "*Isaiah 42:9. God has added to my life a new assignment for the next dimension. He has given me the gift and the anointing for it. *"But as it is written, eye hath not seen, nor ear heard, neither have entered into the heart of man the things which God hath prepared for them that love him. "* I Corinthians 2:9.

My assignment in this chapter is to prepare the body of Christ for the transformation for the next dimension in the spirit. It will be so out of the box, that believers may even question it. This next dimension will be unorthodox Christianity.

The Holy Spirit is preparing the Church for the coming of the Lord. He is not waiting to get the approval from the Apostles, Prophets, Bishops Elders, Pastors, Evangelists, or the Church, asking them what they think concerning this next move! When He does move, I believe it will be a swift one, in spite of all the drama and chaos going on in the world. I also believe that God is revealing this shift (secret) for the next dimension to those who are walking in the presence of the Lord. If you are not seeking the face of God on a daily basis, you may have reservations and or questions when you see the next move of God. *"Surely the Lord God will do nothing but he revealeth, his secret unto his servants the prophets."* Amos 3:7.

For your next dimension, God is strategically connecting the dots in the spirit for your life and bringing you to that place so you can fulfill His purpose. This next dimension is not about you, but it is about His purpose. God is going to bring someone across your path that will open the door and usher you into the next dimension. You can be in the right place, but at the wrong time. This is the season that God is connecting the dots, taking you through the process, and bringing you into the company of people that you need to know. The law of the next dimension will be manifested in your life. It will be the hour of divine connection. So people of God get in the place where you're supposed to be. When you do this, you will bloom where you are planted.

When you get in the place where God wants you to be; you will have promotion and favor. Everything that was against you will begin working for you. God is going to connect you with a person or persons to fulfill His perfect plan. It will be the next dimension for you. Don't become discouraged when people exit your life. Remember when God wants to bring increase to you; he will add a person to you. When He wants to protect you, He will subtract a person from you.

Many would like to know, what is next for the church? Is the church of Jesus Christ necessary? What changes is the church making? Some think that the church is obsolete. It appears that the church does not have influence or power anymore. The light in the temple has just about gone out. *"And ere the lamp of God went out in the temple of the Lord, where the ark of God was."* I Samuel 3:3. The devil is trying to silence the voice of the church through legislation. He is diluting the word of God, from which we amplify our Christian faith. He is adding to and taking away from the Bible; changing its very wording. If this was done to the Koran, Muslims everywhere would rise up and demand a change!

There is an attempt to silence Christians in America. Whether you want to believe it or not; there are evil spirits behind certain legislation. These spirits are called principalities. They have influenced the government to pervert natural laws. Judges are overturning the vote of the people, because their voices are in disagreement with certain sexual preferences. Judges are saying that this is discriminating and unconstitutional. Really, the bottom line is they are anti-God and anti-Christ. These judges are trying hard to overthrow the foundation of good morals, and the voice of the people, by changing laws and legislative polices. This puts the church at a cross road, whether she is going to be politically correct or whether she will agree with sound doctrine and truth. The enemy is really trying to silence the Church's freedom of speech.

How did the church of Jesus Christ become lukewarm? I'll tell you how. One; there is a lack of prayer, and two;- the church has compromised truth. When you mix a little bit of truth, with a little bit of error it always equals compromise. Truth should never be compromised. The American church has exalted government above truth. In the African-American community, we celebrated the very first African-American President of the United States of America. After all these years, and all of the racial, prejudice abuse that the Black race has suffered; it was good to see that a black man was finally going to the white house. To be honest with you, I thought I would have never seen this. I pray constantly for the President and his family.

I would like to say that the election of the first African American president of the United States of America was an act of the sovereignty of God. Why do I say that? In Daniel chapter two, verse 21 it says *"and he changes the times and the seasons; he removeth the kings and setteth up kings, he giveth wisdom unto the wise and knowledge to them that knoweth understanding"*. Remember in the beginning of chapter two, I said God is as sovereign as his word. The reason why we are seeing our nation, governments and churches in such turmoil is because the church has become lukewarm. Now, our government and nation has kicked God to the curb. The local church has even evicted Jesus and his principles from the Church. *"Behold I stand at the door and knock: If any man hear my voice and open the door I will come into him and sup with him and he with me". Revelation 3: 20.*

If we're going to preserve this nation, for our children children's children and generations to come . We must not ever forget God. *For the Lord is our judge, the Lord is our lawgiver, the Lord is our King he will save us".* Isaiah 33:22. We must not ever forget God nor His principles, or it will not go well for America.

Our judges have exalted government policies above godly principles. When government goes against the principles of God, the church should never compromise principles of truth in order to embrace any policy of government. The church that preaches holiness should never turn around and endorse or vote for any political candidates that oppose godly principals. God is not going to skip over the church house to deal with the white house!

First, we are not called to be democrat, republican, independent, conservative, or liberal. We are called to be Holy. I know Holy is a word that you don't hear much anymore. When you believe in holiness, you will not back or enforce any political party, racial platform or sexual agenda, because you're a citizen of the Kingdom of Heaven. The church has become lukewarm because we have compromised truth. It is diluted because of a mixture of truth and error.

Truth should never be diluted. It should never be sacrificed or compromise for any political, sexual or racial platform. Truth should be esteemed above all. *"Neither have I gone back from the commandment of his lips: I have esteemed the words of his mouth more them my necessary food."* Job 23:12. When people fall away from truth, it opens the door to what you are seeing today.

The church was not birth to be politically correct. The church was birth to seek and to save that which is lost through the Holy Spirit. The church is the light of the world, above religion and politics. The church is still in charge of this earth. *"If my people, which are called by my name, shall humble themselves, and pray, and seek my face, and turn from their wicked ways; then will I hear from heaven, and will forgive their sin, and will heal their land."* II Chronicles 7:14.

The church is a reflection of God in the earth. It is still the most powerful and purposeful institution on earth. The church is not obsolete, she is still necessary. I want everyone to know that God is not finished with the church. God is really just getting started. People are asking, What is God's answer to all the evil that is going on in the world? Where is God? What is God going to do about it? God has already done everything that needs to be done. Jesus said, *"it is finished."* John 19:30.

First, let's get something straight, God is not on the defense, He's always on the offense. He's not counter acting to any of the attacks on our foundation and freedom. *"Woe unto them that call evil good and good evil: that put darkness for light, and light for darkness: that put bitter for sweet, and sweet for bitter!* Isaiah 5: 20. In today's church, what use to be wrong, is now considered permissible, and ok, what use to be right is now wrong.

"If the foundations be destroyed, what can the righteous do?" Psalms 11:3. God didn't send the solution when there was an attack on our foundation. His solution to the foundation problem was already given before there were any attacks. I believe that the next move of God, which is the next dimension of His glory, will be totally out of the box. We know the glory of God to be the physical manifestation of the presence of God. Out of the box means nothing of the norm. It will not be church as usual. God has released a glory and a grace for this season of dimension. It will draw the most unlikely people to Him. The Holy Spirit is preparing the Church for the great outpouring in the next dimension. We will see creative miracles, signs, and wonders. In this next dimension of glory, there will be undeniable miracles.

The next dimension is going to baffle the orthodox, and put a bitter taste in the mouths of those who are stuck in religion. To all of you who just go to church, but are not really interested in seeing and getting souls saved and delivered. You're going to miss this divine visitation of the Holy Spirit. Jesus was the seed planted, so that God would receive this great end time harvest.

For this next dimension the Holy Spirit is developing a culture of people who are sensitive to His voice, know the working of His mighty power, are open to how God will be operating. This is how God will reach this end time harvest. The mantle of the Holy Spirit is falling.

We must be sensitive to the voice of the Holy Spirit. The out of the box glory that I'm speaking of, are the things that God will be doing to reach lost souls in these last days. *"Ask of me, and I shall give you thee the heaven for thine inheritance and the uttermost parts of the earth for thy possession."* Psalms 2:8.

On December 28, 2009, my wife and I attended a camp meeting service in Cape Girardeau, Missouri at the Christ Church of The Heartland with my good friend Pastor Zach Strong. A young man by the name of Prophet Brian Carn was ministering on that night. I know that many of you don't believe in the prophetic. However, on this particular night, while in worship, my wife and I were sitting on the front row. "Who is Maurice?" he said. I replied, "I'm Maurice. He looked at my wife and said;" The people call you Sister Williams, what do they call you?" She replied "Sister Williams." He went on to tell me what I needed to change so I wouldn't suffer the things that the men in my family had suffered. He also said some other things to me. This was a prophetic word to me. The word that he spoke began preparing me for this season that I'm in. God gave me a little over a two and half-year window; before having the AVM and the losses. He did not allow the AVM to sneak up on me.

God is raising up men and women for the end time glory. God has preserved a remnant for himself; who are not politically correct, nor religious but walking in truth. They will usher in His glory in an unorthodox way. If you try to usher in this next dimension in your own strength and power, it could destroy you. We can still bring about a change, in our culture and this generation.

"When the master of the feast had tasted the water that was made wine and did not know where it came from but the servants who had drawn the water new, the master of the feast call the bridegroom and he said unto him every man at the beginning sets out the good wine and when the guest have well drunk then the inferior; you to have kept the good wine until now!" John 2:9-10.

God has preserved the good remnant wine for last. God knows exactly what it will take to reach this end time harvest. He also knows how to bring revival to the body of Christ. I believe that I am one of the many that God has preserved for the next move of spiritual outpouring. The devil's assignment was to try to keep me from entering into this next dimension. His main objective was to kill me, by taking me out prematurely."The thief cometh not, but for to steal, and to kill, and to destroy: I am come that they might have life, and that they might have it more abundantly." John 10:10.

God set a miracle in motion for me; His grace was a disruption against what the enemy tried to do. The enemy assignment backfired. If he knew, the good that was going to come out of this, he never would have messed with me. *"Which none of the princess knew: for had they known it, they never would have crucified the Lord of glory."* 1 Corinthians 1:8. God is ushering me into the realm of the unknown. This next dimension of end time glory was hid in God before the foundations of the world. God is revealing this next dimension to us by His Spirit.

No one ever seen or heard anything like this. Never so much as imagine anything quite like it. What God has arranged for those who love Him. However, you've seen and heard it because God by his spirit has brought it all out into the open before you. The spirit, not content to flit around on the surface, dives into the depths of God, and brings out what God planned all along. I Corinthians 2:9-10 *Message Bible.*

Your spirit must perceive this next move of God. This perception will only come to you by way of revelation and discernment. It carries a certain sound of what God is about to do. *"And Elijah said unto Ahab, Get thee up,*

eat and drink: for their is a sound of abundance of rain."
I Kings 18:41.There was a drought for over three and
one- half years. Before it began to pour down raining,
Elijah heard it in the realm of the spirit. Once you
perceive it in your spirit, it will not be long before you
will see it. Every believer must be in tune with the Spirit
of God to hear this sound for the next dimension.

The church is experiencing a spiritual drought. The
drought is so severe that it has produced famines that are
subtracting from truth and the miraculous. The reason
why there has been such a drought is that there hasn't
been any rain of glory. There is a famine of the word of
God, a famine of his presence, principles, purpose and of
His spirit. What use to be wrong is now permissible, and
what use to be questionable, has been desensitized so
that now it is considered ok. There is a remnant that is
hungry and thirsty for the things of God. If you haven't
noticed, there has been a shift of the presence of God
from America to different places like in parts of Africa,
and South America etc. There was a time when America
was producing and sending missionaries all over the
world. Now other countries are sending missionaries to
America to introduce Jesus to the people in America.

We are about to see the greatest outpouring of the Spirit
of God that we have ever seen. We are coming to the end
of this age. This next dimension will be totally out of the
box. God is rising up people who you wouldn't even
expect for him to use. God loves souls.

God will do whatever it takes, to reach the lost, even if He has to go outside the norm to get it done. I am telling you right now. Get ready because this outpouring will be out the box.

Reading about the life of Jesus, I discovered Him to be the most unorthodox, controversial, person ever. He confronted evil on all levels. He was a revolutionist. Jesus was not afraid of the religious system, or the political system of his day. He would purposely heal people on the Sabbath day, which was unlawful with the religious system. He would break all the rules to achieve his objective.

When Jesus made choice of His disciples, he didn't choose any from the Sanhedrin, nor those of the religious sect. There was a reason Jesus did not choose men who had religious backgrounds. He came to establish the Kingdom of God. He was against religion. This is why He had to go outside of the system when making his selection.

Jesus selected twelve men to be His disciples, and he saw a hope in them of not being conformed to a religious box. In His selection, he went outside the box. He made choice of fishermen, a gang member, tax collector and those who didn't have a favorable past. The men that Jesus handpicked were far from being spiritual giants or role models. None of them had any previous background as a Rabbi. Me personally I would have never made choice of these twelve men to meet my objective. God sees in you what nobody else can see.

Jesus saw in them, what no one else could see. *"At about that same time he climbed a mountain to pray. Jesus was there all night in prayer before God. The next day he summoned his disciples and among them he selected twelve as apostles;"*

o Simon who was named Peter,
o James,
o John,
o Phillip,
o Bartholomew,
o Matthew,
o Thomas,
o James, Son of Alpheus,
o Simon called the Zealot,
o Judas, Son of James,
o Judas Iscariot, who betrayed him.   *Luke 6: 12-16*

Jesus made choice of a publican, gang-banger, and businessmen to walk and minister with him. Can you imagine that, a publican, gang-banger ministering with Jesus? Tax collectors cheated the common people. They were considered the enemy. The Roman government was also considered the enemy. Rome employed publicans. It was legal for them to cheat the people. For example, if you were unable to pay your taxes, the tax collector then would loan you the money with interest. He would also set his own fee. If you were still unable to pay, the tax collector had the power to put you in jail. This is one reason why they were hated.

"And after these things he went forth and saw a publican, named Levi, (Matthew) sitting at the receipt of custom: and He said unto him, follow me. And he left all rose up and followed him." Luke 5:27-28. Matthew turned around and threw a big party and guess what? Jesus attended the party. There were many ungodly people there. Jesus attending the party was totally out of the box for religion.

"But their scribes and Pharisees, murmured against his disciples, saying, Why do ye eat and drink with publicans and sinners? And Jesus answering said unto them, They that are whole need not a physician; but they that are sick. I came not to call the righteous, but sinners to repentance." Luke 5:30-32.

When you're out of the box you will become a target of the insecure. Insecure people are fueled by fear. They are inferior of someone or something because they don't know who they are. "I've said it before and I'll say it again, what you don't understand you will fight." Jesus was not concerned about what the religious leaders thought of him, because he knew that he was the Christ the Son of the living God.

When you know that, you are the righteousness of God in Christ. You have a position of superiority and mastery over the devil. *"Behold I give unto you power to tread on serpents and scorpions, and all the power of the enemy: and nothing shall by any means hurt you."* Luke 10:19. You don't care about their negative vibes, negative words, or negative things that may be coming at you, because you know who you are. You know your identity. True identity can only be discovered in Christ. Only He who created you can give you, your identity.

Let's look at this gang member; Simon the Zealot who was chosen to be an Apostle. The Zealots were an anti-government, anti-religious group. They hated those systems. It is believed that Barabbas was a member of this gang. He committed murder during the uprising against the Roman government. *"And there was one named Barabbas, who was chained with his fellow rebels; they had committed murder in the rebellion."* Mark 15:7 Can you imagine Jesus choosing a gang banger to walk and minister with him?

There may have been a strong possibility that Simon could have also been a murderer. No doubt, the Zealots robbed the rich to give to the poor. The Zealots hated Herod, Caesar, Pilot, tax collectors, publicans, Roman soldiers, and anyone that was associated with the Roman government. They would rob, steal, kill, and destroy, anything that was associated with Rome.

I believe that Matthew was the most disliked out of all the disciples because of his past. Matthew taxed fishermen every time there was a large catch. He would heavily tax and cheat the hard working men. Jesus made choice of a publican, a gang member, and fishermen, along with others, and made them part of His circle. By Matthew being a tax collector, he had a connection with the chief publican Zacchaeus.

The Roman soldiers would go into homes at will, take food, and rape many Jewish women; they were not held accountable for their actions. This fueled hatred in the Jewish community. The religious leaders taught the people a doctrine that it was ok to hate. The people believed the doctrine because it came from the religious leaders. Jesus began teaching the doctrine of agape love. This upset the religious system. *"Ye have heard that it hath been said, thou shalt love thy neighbor, and hate thine enemy."* Matthew 5:43. *"But I say unto you, love your enemies, bless them, that curse you, do good to them that hate you, and pray for them which despitefully, use you, and persecute you:* Matthew 5:44

Jesus did not fit or looked the mold of what the Messiah should be. He was just a natural, common, ordinary man. Ungodly people constantly surrounded him. He was God in the flesh, known as the friend of sinners. The people who were drawn to Jesus were those who felt that they were not good enough for the synagogue, temple, or religious system, because of their sinful issues. The disciples whom Jesus chose to work with him were rough around the collar. He was seen in public walking down the street with women who had terrible history.

"And certain women which had been healed of evil spirits and infirmities, Mary called Magdalene, out of whom went seven devils, and Joanna the wife of Chua Herods, steward, and Susanna, and many others which ministered unto him of their substance." Luke 8:2-3. Many ungodly people loved being in the presence of Jesus.

He spoke the language of the people. For example when He was around farmers, he would say things like *"a sower went to sow or when He was around fishermen He would say,"* the kingdom of heaven is like a net that was cast into the sea and gathered of every kind. Which when it was full, they drew to shore, and sat down, and gathered the good into vessels, but cast the bad away."* Matthew 13: 47-48. Jesus spoke to the people on their level. He could relate to the people about things they understood.

My question to the body of Christ is, are you ready for this next dimension of glory? Remember it will be out of the box. We are about to see the greatest out pouring we have ever seen. I know it doesn't look as if there is going to be a latter glory dimension, because of the influence of evil that is seen throughout the world. I have no doubt that the Holy Spirit is getting the church prepared for this next dimension. He is sanctifying and washing the church with the water of the word, *"that Jesus may present it to himself a glorious church, not having spot, or wrinkle, or any such thing; but that it should be Holy and without blemish."* Ephesians 5:27. Jesus will return soon to receive His Church. We are about to see the greater works that Jesus promised that we would do.

"Ye are the salt of the earth: but if the salt has lost his savour, wherewith shall it be salted? It is thence forth good for nothing, but to be cast out, and be trodden under foot of men. Matthew 5:13. Don't fall victim to this notion that it's all over for the church. Some may even believe the church is good for nothing.

Come on church! We are the salty remnant that makes others thirsty for what we have. We also give flavor to every bland situation. Salt is also a preservative. The church is preserving all creation. *"For the earnest expectation of the creature waiteth, for the manifestation of the sons of God."* Romans 8:19 *"For we know that the whole creation groaneth, and travaileth, in pain together until now."* Romans 8:22.

Don't just lie down and surrender your godly principals, and then say come quickly Lord Jesus and rapture us up out of this mess. Stand up for what you believe. There is this notion that the church is obsolete, void of power and influence. I want to go on record and say that the church has a voice and she still has influence. The church has not seen her best days. Jesus is coming for a glorious church. He is not coming for a church that has given up on His vision, or who have abandoned the cause of the ministry.

God has allowed me to come back to minister in this next dimension. Since I did not die, that means I am relevant for this hour. There is still unfinished business that I need to take care of. I still have a purpose. God also left you in the earth, to fulfill that purpose which is going to make a difference. We are that church that Jesus is coming for. Therefore, we must rise in power to become that glorious church. We are faced with things we have never been confronted with before.

One of the most unforgettable scriptures in the Bible in my opinion is Judges 2: 10. *"And all that generation we're gathered unto their fathers and their arose another generation after them, which new not the Lord, nor yet the works which he had done in Israel."* The church must be relevant for this generation and this society. The church cannot be obsolete!

Why didn't that generation know the Lord or any of His miraculous works? It was because the father's did not teach their children the word of God nor did they rehearse in their ears the miracles of God. This sounds familiar! If revelation of the word is not taught, it will be lost! If the word is not taught, there will be no reverence for the Lord. Generations will wax worse and worse and society will become desensitized to good morals.

Generations and societies as we know them will always change for the worse. The Spirit of wisdom will show us how to reach the people of this society and generation. We are confronted with some things that we have never had to face before as follows:

- o Same sex pastors,
- o Islamic radical militants,
- o The sagging generation,
- o The Fatherless generation,
- o Body piercing generation,
- o A wicked and perverse generation
- o Stay at home dad generation,
- o Same sex marriage generation,
- o Same sex adoption of children,
- o Homosexual generation,
- o Lesbian generation,
- o Cashless generation,
- o The down-low generation,
- o A young generation of inmates,
- o A faithless and perverse generation.

I know you are asking why homosexuality and lesbianism surfaced like it has. This perversion is very bold and it has no shame. Perversion is coming out of the closet while the Christians are going into the closet and keeping silent. I believe one of the reason why we are seeing an increase in homosexuality, is because the soon coming world ruler the anti-christ will also be a homosexual. *"Neither shall he regard the God of his father's, nor the desire of women, nor regard any god:*

for he shall magnify himself above all." Daniel 11:37. The majority of the courts are in favor of the alternative lifestyle. When the antichrist appears, homosexuality will seem to be a normal way of life. The anti-christ will have no resistance.

In spite of the courts controversial rulings concerning same sex marriages, the church must love and show love without compromising the truth. *"For God so loved the world, that he gave his only begotten son that whosoever believeth on Him should not perish but have everlasting life.* John 3:16. God loves souls.

The young people of this generation have no regards for life. They don't mind dying. Life for them is not in their vision. When they have children, they do not teach their children about life. You cannot teach what you do not possess. When they are sentenced to 10-15-20-25 years, or life without parole, it seems to be nothing to the young people of today. We have a generation and a society of the walking dead.

These guys are falling into mass deception, such deception has incarcerated them. The incarcerations have prevented many young men from marrying and producing children.

Sexual perversion such as homosexuality and lesbianism prevents the human seed from reproducing. The male carries the seed. There is a spirit that wants to kill, steal and destroy the male and their seed. If you take the man out of the equation, you take away generations. I call this the modern extermination of the male seed. We have seen this spirit in manifestation and operation before. *"And Pharaoh charged all his people saying, every son that is born ye shall cast into the river, and every daughter ye shall save alive "*. Exodus 1 : 22.

Some of the young men that are in the gangbanging lifestyle already know they are not going to live to be old. Therefore, they are going to the mortuary paying cash for their funeral service. It is a shame that they are choosing to die at such a young age. When I was growing up as a child, young people were not dying as they are today.

I want to go on record and say that parents have abandoned their responsibilities by not parenting, as they should. *"Train up a child in the way he should go: and when he is old, he will not depart from it."* Proverbs 22: 6. Today's children have no structure, discipline, or boundaries. It is so sad that children today are left to raise themselves. There is nothing wrong with you as a parent saying to your child no. It is time to be their parent, instead of trying to be their best friend. You are to protect them, and make the right decisions for them, because they are too young to make any mature and adult decisions.

In today's society, many of the young men had no father growing up. This is one reason they grow up soft, coming from a single parent home. Don't get mad at me, I'm only giving you the truth. These young guys have never baited a hook, never gotten dirty while playing; they don't know how to put oil in a car. They don't go outside to play. They sit inside the house and play video games day and night. They are not use to any type of labor. There is a spirit that is working to do away with any type of masculinity! You can see it in fashion, entertainment, etc.

The majority of mothers have spoiled their sons, and the sons have adopted their mother's personality. They have become feminized. These small things have affected our society. When men grow up soft, young women have no strong men to marry. Many of the young men of this society really don't want a wife. This is the beginning of the breakdown of the family. If the foundation of the family has any type of crack in it, there will be a moral decay of society. *"For the man is not of the woman but the woman of the man neither was the man created for the woman but the woman for the man."* I Corinthians 11:8-9. God said he created woman for man.

In Bible customs, every Jewish boy was given a trade by his father. With this trade, it opened the door for economic opportunities. It is also the father's responsibility to see the gifts in his children and shoot them into the direction of those gifts, as mighty arrows. *"As arrows are in the hand of a mighty man; So are children of thy youth."* Psalms 127:4. The apostles James and John were fishermen, because they learned the trade from their father, Zebedee. Saul of Tarshish was a tent maker, because he learned the trade from his father. Jesus was a carpenter, because he learned the trade from his earthly father Joseph. These generations of young boys are not equipped for a trade. They want to make a fast buck. They don't want to work. They feel by working, it will take a long time for them to accomplish whatever goals they have.

The devil gives these young people vision, that if they sell drugs they can get rich quick. *"For the love of money is the root of all evil: which while some coveted after, they have erred from the faith, and pierced themselves through with many sorrows."* I Timothy 6:10. What he doesn't show them is how selling drugs will lead to problems. There are only two things this lifestyle leads to, imprisonment, and death. In our society, Fathers are not shooting their children like arrows in the direction of their gifts. Young boys are not guided to a trade or education for economic opportunities. Fathers today really don't know how to be fathers; because they were never fathered themselves.

The times of our society in which we now live are changing every day. The change that we are seeing is not for the better. Therefore, the church cannot afford to be irrelevant in this hour. We may change our methods whereby we minister, without ever changing the message. Again, the church must know how to minister to this generation and this society. The message is not an event, it is not a thing, but it is about the person Jesus, and having a personal relationship with him! That is the message! We must approach this society with the Holy Spirit's message and methods in order to persuade them to the Lord. His message will never change, but His methods will change. Water is a symbol of the Holy Spirit. *"In the last day that great day of the feast Jesus stood and cried saying if any man thirst let him come unto me and drink he that believeth on me as the scripture has said, out of his belly shall flow rivers of living water."* John 7:37-38. River water flows downstream. It is never stagnant. Living waters minister with new methods, to every society and every generation.

You cannot use methods from 10 years ago, to accomplish your objectives for today. The Holy Spirit is always moving and producing methods, that are relevant for every season, generation, and society. This next dimension is preceded by a sound. How and what does it sound like? The sound for the next dimension is a strong hard-core, militant sound. It is not a soft, prissy, harp, mellow type of sound. In this hour, you can't be passive, apathetic, or nonchalant. *"The kingdom of heaven suffereth, violence and the violent take it by force."* Matthew 11: 12.

I want to prepare you for what you're about to see with your natural eyes. I believe that what's about to happen is a Holy Ghost revival; promotion and supernatural favor coming to the people of God, just as He promised He would. Jesus is going to reveal himself to those who have no church affiliation. *"The woman saith unto him. I know that Messiah cometh, which is called Christ; when he is come, he will tell us all things. Jesus saith unto her, I that speak unto thee am he."* John 4: 25-26. We're about to see revival in the Muslim and Jewish cultures. It's taking place even now.

Jesus is revealing Himself to those who don't look, dress, or smell like you think a person should. God will deliver one from among them, then go back and get the rest of them. I believe that God will reveal Jesus to everyone someway, somehow to either except or reject Him. "Jesus said unto him I am the way, the truth, and the life: no man cometh unto the Father, but by me." John 14:6. I believe that everyone will have an opportunity to either except or reject Jesus. It is not within our judgment to say who is going to make it, and who is not. *"For the grace of God that bringeth, salvation hath appeared to all men."* Titus 2:11.

I invited a former Muslim who converted to being a believer in Jesus, to speak at our church; Dr. Nasir Siddiki. Dr. Siddiki is a traveling evangelist and conference speaker. He told our church that he was in the hospital dying of shingles, when a man walked in his hospital room and said, *"I am the God of Abraham, Isaac, and Jacob."* The man turned around and walked out. Dr. Siddiki said the man did not preach Jesus to him but it was what he said, and how he said it, which caused him to seek Jesus. "So I began reading the Bible and discovered Jesus said Dr. Siddiki. He began to cry out to the Father in the name of Jesus. He confessed Jesus as Savior and Lord. He renounced Islam and embraced Jesus.

In this next dimension, the church of Jesus Christ will see and do supernatural things. If you are not in tune with the Holy Spirit, it will look weird to you. We are about to see creative miracles and also the former gang banger, homosexuals, and lesbians who have been delivered by the power of the Lord Jesus Christ. Many others will go forth in God with their dreadlocks and tattoos to fulfill the great commission. They will not look for a platform. Those coming to Christ will not be concerned about a title. Their true concern will be to see heaven invade the earth. *"Thy kingdom come, Thy will be done in earth, as it is in heaven."* Matthew 6:10.

In this next dimension, the church of Jesus Christ will manifest the glory of God through legislation, and by getting on their knees overturning ungodly policies in the natural realm. This church will endorse candidates that believe in good morals, traditional marriage, and traditional family values. *"When the righteous are in authority, the people rejoice: but when the wicked bearers rule, the people mourn."* Proverbs 29:2.

There is an attack on our faith and freedom by our very own government. Come on church! We had better rise up! For wicked men to reign is for good men to do nothing. We must fight this good fight of faith. You cannot be comfortable with your faith in this season. It is not time for you to put your faith on cruise control, but it is time to rise up and get in agreement with God's word.

In this next dimension of the church, we will see a remnant walking in power, miracles, signs, and wonders and going after this society and this generation fully to persuade them to become Jesus believers. The Holy Spirit has given the church wisdom to perform the methods in this season to get the job done. Don't be like the Pharisees and those of the religious sect and miss your divine visitation of God; simply because the visitation doesn't look like what you're accustomed to or how/what you think it should be. This visitation will be nothing of the norm. God has a passion for souls. The harvest is ripe and God needs laborers to go and pick the harvest. Did you know that there is a move of the Holy Ghost going on within the Muslim culture? Muslims are being converted to believers in Christ Jesus.

"But where unto shall I liken this generation? It is like unto children sitting in the markets and calling unto their fellows, and saying we have piped unto you, and ye have not danced: We have mourned unto you, and ye have not lamented. For John came neither eating nor drinking and they said He hath a devil. The son of man can neither eating and drinking, and they say, behold a man

gluttonous, and a winebibber, a friend of publicans and sinners. But wisdom is justified of her children." Matthew 11: 16-19. Again, this next dimension of glory will be totally out of the box. Remember, it will not be Christianity as usual.

About the Author

Pastor Maurice Williams

Pastor Williams has been in the ministry over 30 years preaching and teaching the good news. Pastor Maurice Williams has a very diverse background in ministry. He has served as teacher, leader, evangelist, outreach, Associate Pastor and Senior Pastor. God has truly anointed him to love with a purpose of building families, encouraging, empowering and developing broken people. A Bible teacher, preacher and disciple maker, Pastor Williams is committed to show the masses the power and the authority of the Holy Spirit to transform and reconcile the world.

Pastor Maurice Williams accepted his call to ministry on March 22, 1981 at the age of nineteen. He began his journey in the ministry at the Macedonia Missionary Baptist Church of Kansas City, Kansas, under the pastoral leadership of the late Pastor O. L. Cobbins, Sr. Pastor Williams is a graduate of the Harvest Bible Institute, Kansas City, Missouri. Pastor Williams is the Founder/ Senior Pastor of Church Triumphant World Overcomers International in Kansas City, Missouri. Under his leadership, the church grew and moved into a new building in 2004. He has preached many revivals and conferences throughout the country. Pastor Williams is the founder of Maurice Williams Ministries and creator of the daily radio show, "*Taking You to Another Level*". His program and ministry were regularly featured on the TBN, Praise the Lord network.

Pastor Williams is happily married to his lovely wife Holly, and five beautiful children: Monique Roberts, Mikayla Williams, Mishael Williams, Menellus Williams and Haley Williams.

For a copy of this book or to invite Pastor Maurice Williams to speak at your church or event,

Contact Maurice Williams Ministries via:

Email: mwilliams5337@gmail.com

Office: 816-804-7906

Online: www.MauriceWilliams.org

Write: Pastor Maurice Williams
PO Box 27047
Overland Park, Kansas 66225

End Notes

[1]American Stroke Association, Impact of Strokes, http://www.strokeassociation.org/STROKEORG/AboutStroke/Impact-of-Stroke-Stroke-statistics_UCM_310728_Article.jsp, Accessed November 21, 2014

[2] Skandalon is a Greek word defined as "the name of the part of a trap to which the bait is attached, hence, the trap or snare itself, as in Rom 11:9, from Vine's Greek Dictionary, http://gospelhall.org/bible/bible.php?search=skandalon&dict=vine&lang=greek, Accessed November 25, 2014

All scriptures are taken from the King James Version, New King James Versions of the Bible and The Message Bible.

22577084R00099

Made in the USA
San Bernardino, CA
12 July 2015